D0518508

The Secret Surfer

IAIN GATELY was raised in Hong Kong and studied law at Cambridge. He is the author of four books including *La Diva Nicotina: The Story of How Tobacco Seduced the World*, *Drink: A Cultural History of Alcohol* and *Rush Hour: How 500 Million Commuters Survive the Daily Journey to Work*. He lives in Dorset with his partner, Vanessa, and their family.

The
Secret
Surfer
Iain Gately

An Apollo Book

Leabharlanna Poibli Chathair Baile Átha Cliath

Dublin City Public Libraries

This is an Apollo book, first published
in the UK in 2018 by Head of Zeus Ltd

Copyright © Iain Gately, 2018

The moral right of Iain Gately to be identified as the author
of this work has been asserted in accordance with the
Copyright, Designs and Patents Act of 1988.

All rights reserved. No part of this publication may be reproduced,
stored in a retrieval system, or transmitted in any form or by any
means, electronic, mechanical, photocopying, recording, or
otherwise, without the prior permission of both the copyright
owner and the above publisher of this book.

9 7 5 3 1 2 4 6 8

A catalogue record for this book is available from
the British Library.

ISBN (HB): 9781784974985
ISBN (E): 9781784974992

Typeset by Adrian McLaughlin

Printed and bound in Germany by CPI Books GmbH

Head of Zeus Ltd
First Floor East
5–8 Hardwick Street
London ECIR 4RG
WWW.HEADOFZEUS.COM

Contents

1
Staring at the Sea

We moved to Dorset in November 2014. It was stormy all winter and when some friends visited from London in the new year, we walked to the cliffs at Eype to watch waves crashing onto the shingle beach below.

'Imagine being out there, at sea,' Charles said.

'I've been out there,' I told him.

The invitation to imagine sent my memory whirling: I'd driven sailing boats through Atlantic storms with giant swells collapsing around me into avalanches of foam; I'd paddled out on a surfboard to waves that looked big from the shore and immense when I was among them, lying on my belly and staring at their crests as they turned clear as glass, then shattered and came tumbling down on my head...

'Yes,' said Charles, and frowned. Perhaps he thought I hadn't heard him – or that an act of imagination was beyond me. He cupped his hands around his mouth and shouted, 'Look at the waves,' then stabbed a finger at the sea.

I didn't need to look: I could feel them – feel the ground tremble underfoot as they detonated against the shore, feel the compression in my ears as each blast passed. And it hurt to be standing on a cliff in Dorset, staring at the medium that in turns had made me brave and scared me witless, fielding inane remarks from an old friend who liked his salt water flat, warm, and clear: St Tropez in summer, the Maldives or Barbados in other seasons; who'd dedicated himself to the comforts of life long ago, at the expense of neglecting its challenges.

Like Charles, you can stare at the sea and pretend to be moved, but imagination has its limits. You can't learn much about it from the shore. Even when you're being lashed with spray and horizontal squalls of wind and rain on a cliff top, you're still perched on solid ground, and so insulated from its power and, indeed, vitality. The sea is in constant motion. It flows, rises, spins and judders, and even when its swells are metronomic, as if each were a heartbeat, there are always cross-rhythms that add flickers to its pulse. The glassiest breakers have potholes and bulges on their faces. Tides whirl to and fro beneath flat calms as the oceans follow the pull of the moon. Giant submarine waves, visible only from satellites on clear days, march between the continents in cycles ranging from fourteen days to hundreds of years as the earth spins and bobs around the sun.

Your feelings about the sea change once you've been in it and over it and under it. It's like having a moody and violent lover who teaches you that pain is the price of pleasure, but who's worth the loving nonetheless, and who arouses you in ways that are unimaginable unless you've experienced them.

As we trudged back from Eype towards Sunday lunch, I thought about how I might get back in the sea. Until two years before it had been my playground. Then my left hip started to crumble with osteoarthritis and I lived as a near-cripple for eighteen months. It was bone-on-bone in the socket and when I saw X-rays of the damage, I realized that my body would never heal itself. I had to wait for a hip-resurfacing operation and take the pills in between. That period marked a clear division in my life. I went from being active both in the water and on the land, from surfing, sailing and trekking up mountains, to limping short distances and slumping indoors. I shrank away from physical contact with other people lest they nudged against me accidentally and plunged me into pain.

Defensive behaviour blackened my thoughts: I searched for marks of decay in my friends, to reassure myself that I wasn't leading the pack towards the grave. I delighted when some filled out, slowed down and embraced middle age, as if they'd been seeking it their whole lives. They bought bigger, softer chairs and followed football teams on television with a passion that was disproportionate to either their interest or involvement in the game when young. They also used their children as proxies, deluding themselves that their faculties were still alive, albeit in other bodies, and would tell me with pride how little Simon or India had won the egg-and-spoon race at school, and expect me to congratulate them for the victory as if it had been their own.

My hip was resurfaced in July 2014. Kindly Mr Latham cut through skin and muscle, severed a few tendons, dislocated my joint, whipped the top off my femur, screwed a titanium hemisphere in its place, ground out the socket in my pelvis, cemented a matching metal cup into the bone, reconnected the joint, and stitched up and stapled back together everything he'd disturbed, all within ninety minutes. The operation itself is one of those overlooked marvels of medical science – like pacemakers – that do so much to prolong life or make it pleasant again. A century ago I'd have been doomed to spend the rest of my years as an invalid.

Recuperation was mental as much as physical: over the first six weeks, as I passed from crutches to a single stick and then learned to walk again, I enjoyed a rare spell of objectivity. I had to acknowledge that I was middle-aged – over the hill – and when the ground starts to fall under your feet all is new again. I hadn't felt so uncertain since my teens, when I was on the upward slope, the world was full of a dizzying array of promises and it had seemed that I might ascend forever.

I realized I was faced with two options: the first was to continue the defensive behaviour I'd adopted prior to my operation. Since I was falling apart, surely it was best to avoid anything that might hasten the process? Why not give up, grow fat and resort to passive forms of entertainment and vicarious pleasures? I was frightened, however, of the mental damage such a surrender might cause. Would my mind follow my body into decline? Would I – in the sense of the 'I' behind my eyes – sink into a make-believe world as the grey matter melted? Fantasizing certainly increases as middle age advances: the older you get, the taller your stories. Perhaps this is a rare example of nature being kind, by softening our minds as age withers our flesh. Everybody deserves a splendid past, whether real or imagined. It becomes the substitute for a glorious future when even the most ardent optimist has to acknowledge that their chances of glory have slipped away.

The second option was to behave as if the past two years of pain had been aberrations, and this was more appealing: I wasn't ready to follow the examples of my sedentary friends. I didn't want to put the cork back in the bottle and call it a night. I'd rather act as if I was still on the way up the hill and keep alive some of the dreams I had when I was young, of what I might achieve in life, and perhaps even fulfil them. While many have become impossible, or improbable – I've left it too late to open the bowling for England and it's unlikely that I'll turn quantum physics on its head, or be called up to fight for my country – there's plenty of time yet before senescence and plenty left to achieve, hang onto, or let go of with good grace.

*

I walked to Eype again the next morning, this time alone. The wind had died and the waves were clean, as if God had ruled lines onto the sea. Out of habit, I scanned the beach for a peak that could be surfed, and when I saw a 'V' of white water with its apex pointing at the horizon and its arms opening out towards the shore, I imagined being out there: waiting for the right wave then dropping down its face, carving turns across it and kicking out at the very last instant as it exploded into spray and spume under my feet. I found that I was twitching as I performed these actions in my memory.

I'd loved surfing although I'd never been as good at it before my operation as I hoped. It had seemed that with just a little more time I'd reach a higher level, but then time had run out. In particular, I'd always wanted to be proficient enough to realize a dream that I'd had since my teens, which was to catch a tube. Tubes occur when deep-water swells slam up against a shallow coast. The base of each wave is deflected and its crest pitches forward to create a temporary tunnel along its face. The aim is to ride inside the tunnel as it closes behind you, but before it rolls you up and spits you out onto whatever it is breaking – a sandbar, a stone ledge, or a coral reef.

Most people in the world have seen a picture of a tube, even if they live in a city a thousand miles distant from any coast. The image of a surfer tucked under the lip of a breaking wave is a twenty-first-century icon, used to sell soft drinks, credit cards, beer, aftershave and toothpaste.

It appeals across cultures and creeds. It suggests independence, vigour and hygiene. It also has a hint of mysticism:
the surfer might be a saint alone in a deep-blue sky, and the
tube their route to Heaven.

Tubes are more difficult to ride than the surfers pictured
inside them suggest. You can't just borrow a board and go
and catch one on your first day out – unless one catches
you and breaks your bones. They are, moreover, short-lived
thrills: the world record for time spent inside a tube is
about thirty seconds. Most rides last between two and ten
seconds, or about the same as a male orgasm. The experience
is said to be spiritual as well as carnal. According to the
Hawaiian surfer Gerry Lopez, one of the first generation
to ride tubes and to measure his state of mind when inside
them, the world falls quiet and seems to slow down. 'This
slow-motion sensation, combined with the silence, had me
wondering whether I had entered a different world from
the one outside the tube. The most distinct impression I
experienced inside the tube was a feeling of complete awe.'

My friends who have caught tubes echo Lopez and say
that time inside them is transcendent – time outside time.
Some have even talked of experiencing rebirth, as they
travelled down a liquid tunnel, pulsing with energy, towards
an 'O' of light.

So why not try to catch one now? If time really slowed
down or stopped inside a tube, then perhaps I could steal
a few seconds back from middle age: pause time's arrow
mid-flight, if only for the space of a single heartbeat? It was

a dizzying challenge. I sat down on the turf at the top of the cliff and weighed it up in my mind. It would be a quest with a goal but without a timetable, and carried out within the limitations of family life. I didn't have the money to pay for a dedicated expedition, with expert hands guiding me towards the perfect wave, or the time to skip off to Australia or Bali for a year and live in a hut behind a beach. It would be an affair of cold seas, clammy wetsuits and messy swells rather than the idyllic version of surfing pictured in adverts. And it wouldn't be easy. Even assuming I regained fitness and balance and pushed my skills to a level I'd never yet reached, I might not find a tube to catch, for they're both rare and fickle. A surfing break might grind out tubes all day every day for a week, then remain calm for a year. And at that break you might have to be in a single square yard of water, travelling at precisely the right speed, to catch one when it appeared, and this virtual window would be a moving target, which opened for a split second then rolled up and vanished if you arrived too late.

There was also the little matter of heart: I'd have to fall before I flew, and surfing hands out beatings to its aficionados when they err, bruising their bodies, flooding their lungs with seawater, blowing out their eardrums and snapping their spines. The anticipation of pain, or the wish to avoid suffering it, was a real obstacle. I'd learned – by trial and error – how to pick a path around it, how to have fun without tears and how to save heartbeats for pleasure rather than wasting them on fear. I'd have to trust the doctors that my new titanium hip joint would bed in and the bone grow over it like a tree's roots around a stone. Rather than worrying that the least impact might wreck this delicate arrangement of flesh and artifice, plunge me into agony and send me back to crutches, I'd have to push on and test its limits while the rest of me was sound.

There was much to be won: I wanted to re-experience the elation one feels offshore where the ocean meets the coast and the waves are rolling in. I wanted to enjoy once again the sheer physicality of surfing. The experience is wet, cold, vibrant and loud. It's like wrestling a shape-shifting giant that wraps itself around you and holds you down, or unrolls itself into an emerald runway that you glide over with foam at your heels, forgetting – for perhaps a millisecond – that you're a slave to gravity.

I also had unfinished business to settle with my adolescent self. If I could realize one of the ambitions I'd had at an age before my idealism had been tarnished by experience and cynicism, it would add a coherence to my life. Rather than seeing a series of snapshots of other me's when I looked back, which recorded how I'd aged and changed, I'd prove to myself I was still the same dreamer, who'd once seen pictures of surfers riding tubes and said to himself with all the certainty of youth, 'I'll do that one day.'

2
Waxing Up

March 2015

I had two of my old surfboards in a bag on top of the hall cupboard, where they'd been planted when we moved house. They'd spent the prior year – while I was hobbling around and waiting for an operation – stored in a dilapidated garden shed where we'd also kept a lawnmower and bedding for the chickens. When I lifted the board bag down its zip had seized up half open, and withered grass-cuttings and shards of straw rained out.

The boards were stuck to each other inside the bag. I prised them apart to find the wax on their faces had blackened, like the grime on a Spanish ham. They didn't look like the magic steeds of old that had sped me over waves. In contrast to Don Quixote, who had delighted at the sight of his spavined mount and rusting sword, I felt dispirited rather than inspired. Then a logo on one of my boards – *Lost* – reminded me of a conversation I'd had in 2003 with a surfer from Seville, in a bar at Cape Trafalgar, who'd owned the same brand of board. In between many beers, and staring at the barmaid who was so breathtakingly beautiful that neither of us had dared to ask her her name, we'd discussed whether a surfboard, if one felt it had to be placed in the Romantic cannon, was the hero's steed, or his sword? El Cid, the Sevilliano told me, rode Babieca into battle against the Moors, but he slew them with the sword Tizona, and indeed Colada, for the Cid kept a quiver of blades. So, it was the sword.

Whether blades or steeds, when I brushed down my boards, held them in turn and felt their balance through my hands, life seemed to stir in them. Their curves and fins and concaves, shaped to skate over and slice into the faces of breaking waves, reminded me of how they'd felt under my bare feet, how they would twitch and zoom – not always in the direction I'd expected – while carrying me over the surface of the sea. Taking them out of the bag broke a spell. All the while they'd been hidden, their enchantment had been suppressed. Now that they were in plain sight, I couldn't ignore them when I came through the front door. They were reminders of what I used to be, and wanted to be again – and more. I was thrilled. I felt like I'd finished an official period of mourning: of wearing black and never smiling, of having to live in the shadows and envy people who could move without pain. My quest had begun.

My head was in place, my heart was eager but my body wasn't yet ready to start surfing again. My lungs weren't too bad: I'd given up smoking after thirty years in pursuit of

La Diva Nicotina and, though I missed the pleasure, it was a change to be woken up by sunlight rather than a coughing fit. The occasional blackouts that had accompanied the first cigarette of the day, when I'd have to sit down and regulate my breathing, also became memories. Perversely, I missed them too. Biologists have found that the emotions of wanting and liking are controlled by different circuits in our brains. Apparently, we want more than we like, and desire many things but love few. Hence, we can want things we don't like – like smoking – and the wanting becomes obsessive: it's never satisfied, because it has to start all over again the moment it has won its prize and realized that it hates it. Every climax is a setback.

Although my wind was sound, I'd lost the core fitness I'd had more or less continuously since the age of sixteen. This takes a long time to wane, but once it's gone, it's hard to regain – mentally, as much as physically. It hurts to get fit and my mind was wary – and weary – of pain. But there was no way out: if I wished to surf I'd have to do things to myself and engage in activities that I neither wanted nor liked. To prepare for the sea, it wouldn't be enough to go to exercise classes every week and wave kettle bells about or pedal stationary bicycles. Although such activities may challenge and please their devotees, they're not sufficient to propel you out to a surf break or give you the steel that you need when you're being spun underwater and bounced between rocks.

I started my rehabilitation slowly and began with my legs. These had wasted while I waited for my refit and my bottom had vanished. This was a serious problem, as I needed power down there to take off on a wave. So, cliff walks with an ageing and crippled dog formed the first part of my rehabilitation. My companion was Roobarb the lurcher, who broke his left forepaw chasing a deer a few years back. Now that he was eleven – and lurchers don't last – he would start to limp a mile or so into our walks. In his prime he could cross a hundred-acre field uphill at forty miles per hour and pull down a stag; now, a baby rabbit was beyond him.

The coast at Eype where we walked together is up and down but the switchback path along the cliffs was easier going than the shingle on the strand, which grated my joints – real and synthetic – at every step. The path follows a barbed-wire fence, with pasture on one side and overhangs and vertical drops to a no-man's land of mud and rock on the other. Chunks fall off the cliffs each year, forming haphazard terraces and bowls behind the beach. Some of these hold pools fringed with rushes, and waist-high waterfalls caused by streams jetting out of strata in the cliffs, others thigh-deep black mud. I left the path and scrambled down to one to search for fossils, and found a perfect clam shell with a fan of ribs on a slice of shale. It had died a hundred and fifty million years ago, but might have been carved there yesterday. It was curious to be walking on a seabed high above the tide.

When Roobarb and I descended from the terrace to the beach, two plump little boys ran over and shouted, 'Look at the old grey dog!' to one another. They were similar enough to be brothers and a year or so apart in age – I guessed at eight and nine. Their cheeks were flushed crimson from their sprint and they stared up at me, mouths open, waiting to be congratulated on their perception.

In the past, I'd admired the usefulness of dogs as an educational tool. Their lifespans are so much briefer than our own that they expose the children of their owners to both decrepitude and death at accelerated rates. This accustoms them to the inevitable, and the passing of a beloved pet is their first lesson in evanescence. It also, I realized, might breed contempt and encourage bad habits, such as mockery of old age. Roobarb and I turned our backs on them and headed for the footpath home.

I supplemented walking with turns on a wobble board. Despite the promise of its name, a wobble board is a mobility aid that is as popular amongst pensioners as surfers preparing for tubes. Mine – an advanced model – is a 16" pea-green plastic disc moulded onto a hemisphere, which is unstable unless part of its rim is touching the floor. You stand astride it and attempt squats and spins without grounding it or falling off. Wobble boards are best ridden without stimulants. I pulled mine out at a dinner party just after I'd bought it to cries of admiration and a queue formed of people wanting a go. James said everyone should own one so we could play adult Subbuteo, then fell off and gashed his temple the instant after mounting it. He'd made the elementary error of standing upright once he was aboard rather than bending his knees, and did me the favour of reminding me of a golden rule of surfing: 'stand tall and fall, stay low and go'.

My cliff walks and wobble board gave me back my bottom.

The next challenge on the road to fitness was agility. When you take off on a wave, you need to be able to spring from a prone position onto your feet in a single movement. This fundamental manoeuvre is called a 'pop up' and must be performed fluently and without any hesitation. Like so many aspects of surfing, it's composed of a deceptively simple sequence of actions that need to work more or less perfectly every time if you want to catch waves. If you pop up too vigorously you'll leapfrog over the nose of your board and get pounded, and if you're too cautious you'll fall off its tail, get sucked up the wave backwards, then be thrown down and held under. You can practise pop ups on the floor: lie down flat on your stomach, arch your back so that your head and chest are clear of the ground, pretend to paddle by scrabbling with alternate arms, then set your hands a palm's width apart under your armpits, press up with enough force to project your body off the floor, bring your legs forwards through the air, and stand up with bent knees as your feet touch down, the back foot leading by milliseconds, so that you hear two sounds as you land: ta-tum!

My first attempts were disappointing. Although I had vivid memories of being nimble, and could still picture myself performing the cartwheels and handsprings that I'd found so easy when I was sixteen, when I lay down on the bedroom floor and made an experimental spring my body juddered rather than flowed. It was as if not just my hip but also every other joint in my skeleton had been replaced with cogs and gears. I moved in clicks, and these were real as well as imagined: I'd spent two years stooped and limping and my back took its time to straighten up. Every week or so there'd be an audible clunk and I'd feel taller and lighter, as if some ratchet at the base of my spine had been released a notch.

In time, as my agility increased, I could manage slow-motion pop ups and creak to my feet. Once I'd achieved this minor triumph, I looked for guidance as to how to improve the manoeuvre. I found it on the internet – which seemed a miracle of progress: when I started surfing in earnest in 2000, YouTube was still five years in the future, and the notion that you could find videos of people of all ages and both sexes teaching you how to pop up at the click of a mouse would have been deemed insane by all but the prophets of Web 1.1. In 2015, I found hundreds of experts, ranging from pubescent Brazilians to a septuagenarian yoga instructress in California, all eager to show me how to get to my feet on a surfboard. The best was Michael John Frampton, an Australian surf and movement coach who taught with a camera at floor level in a small room with a beige carpet. He'd come over to the lens, lie on his side, prop his head on one hand, and explain the lesson before acting it out. It was intimate, if claustrophobic, and when Michael became a little too intense I'd admire his double-jointed elbows. His method worked as soon as I could do thirty press-ups without coughing and snap my back into an arch like a cat struck by lightning.

I supplemented bottom-building and agility training with swimming. Apart from the month after my operation, I'd never given up swimming. It kept me in touch with water and gave me a freedom of movement that I lacked on land. I had, however, to adopt a new regime, which I cobbled together from the online recommendations of a number of surf fitness authorities, and which was far more demanding than my existing workouts: no more languid single miles but rather miles of sprints. The aim was to get the lactic acid flowing in my muscles and then thrash through the water until they cramped up. Once I was really out of breath and shaking like a jelly I could try a few lengths underwater, which would accustom me to tolerate bursting lungs and blackouts without breathing in. Next up were drills – swimming with only one arm in case you dislocated a shoulder, or fanning yourself along with just your palms in case you broke your back. My gurus all counselled visitors to their pages that, however keen they might be to train, however hard they went for the burn, the pool would not prepare them for the ocean. It was like practising for the hard-knock world in the safety of the womb.

*

I got back into the sea at Church Ope Cove on Portland in May 2015. Ope Cove is accessed by a steep path that passes through the fragments of a Saxon church, a tilted graveyard with skulls and crossbones carved on its headstones, and a ruined Norman castle. There's a tumble of black huts on its white shingle beach, which has ledges showing where recent tides have peaked. Ness, my partner, bought one of the huts in December 2013. It was washed off its foundations a month later during a once-every-sixty-two-years storm and squashed into its neighbours. The huts were winched apart and set back on their foundations but have been tilted slightly off the vertical ever since, like the houses in *The Cabinet of Dr. Caligari*.

Ope Cove has a microclimate. Portland is a tied island connected to the mainland by a shingle spit off Chesil Beach. It points almost due south into the English Channel and the skies seem to part over it, before reforming and emptying themselves of their rain onto Dorset. It can be ten degrees warmer than at Dorchester, a few miles inland. There were wall lizards living under the floor of the hut, which flicked out into the sunshine and froze on the flat white stones under its window, thermo-regulating. There were also bloody-nosed beetles – which resemble black scarabs and drool out a toxic droplet of scarlet fluid when threatened – wandering around the rock garden in front of it. Rosy, our six-year-old daughter, adopted one as a pet on her first visit, and we had to find her a fresh 'Beetroot' and pretend it was the same insect, every time we came back.

The water in the cove is often as clear and blue as the Mediterranean, albeit frigid. It was flat calm when I waded in, dressed in an old, worn and sagging wetsuit I'd dug up in the hut. I took a diving mask and, once I was a few strokes from shore, found myself hanging over a giant, submarine rock pool, with weeds streaming up from the boulders on the seabed and anemones, mussels and winkles in their crevices. The colours were greens and purples, with the odd silver flash from a fish that had turned onto its flanks. As I swam further out, the lateral horizon underwater contracted to a green-grey wall in every direction, with shadows beyond.

I scanned them for movement. The films *Blue Water, White Death* (1971) and *Jaws* (1975) traumatized my generation. I've met people who haven't put a toe in the sea for forty years because they *know* a great white shark is out there waiting for them. My friend Paul told me that his Uncle Kevin stopped going to his local swimming pool in Suffolk, a dozen miles inland, lest one materialize and bite him in half. And Nikki, my sister-in-law, spoke of a fictional cousin – I think she was talking about herself – who had been so affected by a fear of sharks in her teens that she thought one might get her while she was on the loo – exploding out of the U-bend, savaging her buttocks with its serrated teeth and dragging her down...

Sharks *do* appear off Portland. I once saw one just south of its Bill when sailing back from the Azores, which was seven or eight feet long and very definitely a flesheater. It was most likely a porbeagle, a cousin of the great white, which had a dent in it amidships, shaped like the cross section of the bulb on the keel of a racing yacht. Its movements were erratic, with a degree of lateral wobble. The wind was light and, as we ghosted by, I peered under the spinnaker and caught a glimpse of its left eye, projecting a curse – or so it seemed – at sailing vessels in general and me in particular. Porbeagles live for thirty years or more. Marine biologists are in two minds as to whether sharks can remember or not and silent on whether they forget – or forgive – grudges. More recently a local woman, Jeanette Longley, rescued a 'man-sized' blue shark that beached itself in West Bay, only a few miles away. 'I have saved hedgehogs and things like that before but nothing like a shark,' she told the *Daily Mail*.

I made it back ashore alive.

Church Ope Cove was a test of progress. When I'd first limped down there, through the graves around the ruined church on the path to the beach, and stopped to explain the *memento mori* on one to Rosy, my operation was still six months in the future. I told her that under the headstones lay Barbary pirates who'd come to England to steal children like her to sell as slaves in Africa. Thereafter, we'd played hide and seek from the pirates on the way to and from the beach, which bought me time to compose myself and hide my pain. Now, with the operation ten months in the past, and wild garlic shooting up along the path and pagoda-shaped blossoms unfurling on the horse chestnut trees overhead, I could carry her up and down to the hut on my shoulders and take her scrambling over the rocks around the point. If there were waves we'd stand together knee-deep in the sea and I'd lift her over them as they broke. She told me that she wanted a pink surfboard – when she was a big girl – and then we would ride side by side all the way to Africa and rescue the children that the pirates had taken away.

If the board is the sword, then a wetsuit is the armour. My old one had cracked and crumbled while it lay in a locker in the hut, and it leaked at the neck, ankles, armpits and groin when I swam around Ope Cove. Unless you skip off to the tropics, you'll be partially or almost totally encased in neoprene, the tighter the better, most times you surf. The water temperature around the British coast seldom rises beyond eighteen degrees Celsius and in winter, when the swells are best, often struggles to reach double figures. Wetsuits work by admitting a layer of water between your skin and their inner surface. Once your body warms the water up, it serves as insulation – the equivalent of a few extra millimetres of fat. They're beautiful because they let you go to places you couldn't otherwise visit, and horrible because they're prisons: when you stretch, or kick out in them they pull you back and sap your energy. They're great if you wipe out and tumble on a reef as their buoyancy returns you to the surface and their skin saves yours from laceration; they're hell to get into and out of – especially if you're hopping around in a crowded car park, with one leg in and one leg out, and are naked underneath.

I went to Newquay to find my armourer. The town is the soul centre of English surfing and its grimy Victorian and Edwardian streets house emporia of surf supplies. My last wetsuit had been made by Rip Curl, so I went to their shop on Bank Street, which sits between branches of the Yorkshire Building Society and Subway and was like a temple in a slum – a shrine to beautiful waves amidst monuments to mammon. Its roof had been raised above its neighbours' and was curved like an eyebrow. Half the height of the façade beneath was decorated with the corporate logo, which represents a cresting wave. The shop front itself was a wall of tall glass panels, showing wetsuits, boards and semi life-sized posters of surfers crouched in tubes.

Its staff functioned as oracles as well as sales girls and boys. Surfers will perform any work with a smile, however degrading, if it lets them paddle out every day that there's swell. I was given a couple of wetsuits to try on by Mick, whose hair was still damp from a pre-work session. It had been mellow rather than pumping, he told me, big, slow, waves that were jade-green and super-clean.

The wetsuits were zipless, skin-tight, with coloured panels on their sleeves and resembled costumes from Star Trek. You had to follow a strict procedure to get into and out of them. I became distracted, bodged the job, and needed to ask for help. Meanwhile, my pores were sprinkling out sweat and my blubber wobbling. I caught sight of myself in the mirror in the cubicle, trapped and helpless like a fly in a web, and gasped in horror. Was it a magnifying mirror? Where had all that fat come from? I accepted that beer was fattening but I hadn't expected it to fatten me. Mick gave me a considerate smile – the sort used by visitors and medical staff in hospital wards to hide stronger feelings of sorrow, pity and sometimes revulsion – then explained how to untangle myself.

'When you start again,' he said, 'check out the instructions on the label. Follow them and you can't go wrong.'

The instructions were too small to read without glasses – indicative of Rip Curl's target age group – but there were pictures as well as words. My new armour was tighter round the neck than any other wetsuit I'd owned and squeezed a little roll of my new fat out its top beneath my chin. It heated up rapidly as it filled with sweat. This was a good sign: the less comfortable the better. When I paid for it Mick gave me a block of wax from a stack beside the desk, which turned out to be a truly prescient act.

Unless you're Kelly Slater, eleven times World Champion, whom I once saw in a video riding a wave on an inverted kitchen table, you'll need wax to go surfing. I learnt this truth the hard way. When I first bought a surfboard in 2000, I ran straight down to the beach at Tarifa where I lived and tried to jump on, but it shot from my grasp as if it was covered in grease. After a number of failed clutches – like a lover trying to seize his other in a dream – a local strolled over and told me I should try some wax. Fibreglass resin is slippery when wet so you need to rub wax on the top of your surfboard so that you can hold it and ride it without sliding off.

It's easy to become paranoid about wax. You could spend days travelling to a wave and find, when you arrive, that your board is bare and there's none to be had for a hundred miles. Interestingly, instead of exploiting wax-neurosis to promote their wares, the minds of its manufacturers seem trapped in eternal adolescence and prefer to use innuendo: Sex Wax, Far-King Wax and Mrs Palmer and Her Five Daughters Cold Water Surf Wax are common brands offering traction for your 'stick'. Mick gave me Sex Wax. Two hours later I was drawing circles with it on my board.

3
White Water

June 2015

Ness and I had a rare weekend away together – just the two of us, with children and dogs parcelled out for care amongst various relatives. We planned a spot of antiquarianism, followed by a trial surf in Perranporth, and a pleasant night of gentle excess in St Ives. As soon as I'd bought my wetsuit we took a back road out of Newquay in search of the Lost Chapel, said to mark the place where Piran, the patron saint of Cornwall, made landfall in the seventh century.

Our pilgrimage to the chapel had been inspired by a conversation with Jane, a friend of Ness's, an otherwise intelligent and entertaining woman, who believed in geomancy.

'It's full of special energy,' she told us, and spread her hands towards us, as if she was giving us a present. 'You'll feel recharged just by looking at it. Some people say Piran was the real Merlin. It's best in spring of course, and Cornwall isn't really Cornwall anymore, but you'll love it: go, go, go!'

I googled the saint before our trip. Piran had been a healer in his native Ireland but worked one miracle too many when he revived the slain on a battlefield, thus enraging its participants who would now have to fight the same battle all over again. They laid down their weapons, tied Piran to a millstone and tossed him off a cliff into the Atlantic while a gale was raging. But God calmed the tempest and sped his favourite over the waves to England.

If the legend is to be believed, Piran was the first surfer – the first named individual to have travelled over the surface of the sea on a man-made object without using sails, oars or any other artificial means of propulsion. Upon arrival in Cornwall, he stepped off his millstone and started preaching. He made instant converts of the only creatures within ear-shot: 'a fox, a badger and a boar'. These, presumably, spread the word and the Cornish flocked to hear the holy man living in the dunes. They credited him with many miracles and considered him to be the inventor, or discoverer, of how to smelt tin. One night, when praying on his knees beside his fire, Piran saw liquid tin bubble out of its hearthstone and form a shining cross. The next morning, after it had cooled and solidified, he displayed his new metal artefact to the faithful and told them how it had been made. His discovery is celebrated in the Cornish flag – a white cross on a black background, representing the molten tin on the saint's hearth. Piran is also claimed to have been a convivial divine. Tin miners adopted him as their patron and celebrated his fabled bonhomie with a binge over Perrantide – the week leading up to his saint's day on 5 March. The phrase 'as drunk as a Perraner' is still in circulation in Cornwall. Piran passed away in his 206th year when he fell down a well. His bones were recovered and venerated. Exeter Cathedral and Waltham Abbey each secured an arm during the Middle Ages, when the cult of magic relics was in full swing and every acquisition – like a new ride in a fairground park – drew more pilgrims.

The chapel that commemorates Piran's arrival, said to have been built above the millstone that carried him from Ireland to Cornwall, has been submerged under its surrounding dunes several times over the last 1,400 years, hence the 'Lost' in its name. Edwardian conservationists, concerned after it vanished under the sand once again in 1890 that it might one day be lost for good, erected a 'preserving structure' over it, resembling a stone and concrete Nissan hut, with iron gratings over embrasures in its façade.*

Although Jane had explained how to find the chapel, neither Ness or I could remember her directions, except that it lay off a B-road somewhere between Newquay and Perranporth. We drove back and forth for half an hour without any luck. I couldn't spot it on the map and the satnav app

---

* The 'preserving structure' was considered an abomination at the time: according to the antiquarian Dr Dexter, 'If the buried church could speak, she would complain bitterly of the writers who have misunderstood her, of the trippers who have robbed her, of the Church that sold her, and of the enthusiasts who have entombed her in that hideous concrete structure.'

on my iPhone drew a blank. We were about to give up when Ness saw a sign for an ancient monument that had been pushed into a hedge. We turned into the lane it indicated, just as mist streamed in from the coast at cinematic speeds and cut visibility to a few yards. The road forked from time to time and soon we were as lost as our objective.

There were holes in the whiteout and in one of them we met a pretty teenaged girl on a horse at a crossroads, the horse pacing and she frowning. Once she'd calmed her mount, we asked her for directions. The Lost Chapel, she said, was easy to find. Go back down the lane and turn right just after the field with cows in it. Park there, take the second style, go downhill, walk crossways until you hit the gorse... Fuck!

Her horse reared, she swore again, and cantered off into the surrounding cloud.

It was impossible to see beyond the fence posts of the fields along the lanes and whether or not they held cows. We stopped at a lay-by where other cars were parked and set out on foot. The mist swelled and dissolved as we walked. One minute you could just about see your shoes and an embroidery of flowers around them – threads of colour, reds, blues and golds, running through the turf – the next, the air might clear for twenty yards around.

We were walking down a gentle slope, criss-crossed with tracks and dotted with clumps of gorse, when a spaniel bitch appeared and ran over to sniff my ankles. I scratched her ears and when her owner materialized soon after asked him if he knew where the Lost Chapel was. 'It's behind that hill,' he said, and pointed at the invisible feature. Look for white stones – like that one. He pointed into the mist again. Come on, Delilah. Man and dog strode away and vanished.

I searched where he'd indicated and found an oblong block cased in moss beside a path better trodden than the others. The path led to another stone, and another, then a whole series of them. After finding a few more marker stones, I could read the furrows in the paths and pick the right one that led to the next.

The mist thinned again and a cross appeared through a hole in the cloud high up to the left – like a mirage, or a sign from heaven showing the way. We climbed towards it, following the slope of a sand dune, and found it was far closer that it had seemed. It was made of two concrete beams, on a concrete plinth, with no inscription on either cross or base to say why it was there. Maybe the chapel and its protective structure had slipped back under the sands and 'X' marked the spot? I wondered what Jane would say when I told her. Had its energy been exhausted by too much giving? Had the millstone on which it rested been released by God and dragged it down?

A web of paths radiated out from the cross. I took one into the mist, towards the sea, and met two Cornish fishermen. They were both in their twenties, wearing T-shirts, trainers and tracksuit bottoms. Each held a rod in one hand, a can of cider in the other and both were tattooed from wrist to neck. Neither had caught any fish but both were genial despite their lack of luck. They'd never heard of a 'lost' what?

A chapel – a little church, I said. Meanwhile the dune grass started nodding around them – the sea breeze had arrived and chased the mist away.

I heard Ness shouting. She'd found it! She pointed at a crater at the foot of the adjoining dune. It looked like a building site that had been started on then partially demolished with dynamite, as if whoever had caused the damage hated the feature so much that they wanted to demean it rather than erase it – to allow it to live on in a ruined state and disappoint visitors for centuries to come. An information board beside the ruins, sponsored by the local council, explained that it had buried the Oratory of St Piran deliberately in 1980, dug it up again in 2008, then torn down its protective structure in 2014 to enable fresh archaeological excavations. Hence the chunks of concrete strewn around the dunes. These works had been funded by a lottery grant and had commenced with great expectations. It was envisaged that various community activities, topped by 'a momentous St Piran's Day Play' would mark their conclusion and celebrate the deliverance of the chapel from centuries of neglect and abuse. Clearly, something had been lost in realizing the dream.

The remains of the chapel itself at the bottom of the crater were unimpressive: a rectangle of broken walls, stumps of columns and a pair of carved stones at the base of a fallen arch. It may be that it suffered in comparison with the only other place of worship I'd seen before that had spent centuries buried in sand. This had been at Konark in Bengal, whose vast stone temple, built to represent the chariot of the sun god, passed so many aeons underfoot that its existence had receded into a legend involving a crow, a turtle, one of Buddha's teeth and an avatar of Krishna. In the nineteenth century, a typhoon blew it clean and its tiers of pornographic carvings, featuring threesomes, energetic penetration both front and back and thirteen of the coital positions described in the Karma Sutra, were once more revealed to view.

The mist had flown up to the clouds, which had dissolved in turn, allowing the sun to blaze through. We climbed back up to the concrete cross and now had a view south along the length of the bay. There were caravan parks all the way to Perranporth. It seemed incredible that they had been so close, yet invisible. People and dogs were scurrying to and fro between the caravans and the dunes. Clacking sounds, meanwhile, rang out from the chapel. A family had arrived and were throwing stones into the pit.

The view out to sea, in contrast, was inspiring. The water was azure, fading to cobalt towards the horizon. And there was swell: a hundred yards or so offshore, the Atlantic reared up in a series of glassy blue lines that burst into foam as they broke and roared up over the beach. It was the bottom of the tide and time to get out on the water.

We drove to Perranporth ('Piran's Port') and parked on the edge of the town beside the sea. Ness set off to the nearby

Seiners Arms with a sketchbook and the latest Mo Hayden novel. I fought my way into my new wetsuit, grabbed my board and hopped barefoot over the gravel in the car park and down to the beach. I threaded a path through its windbreaks, each of which framed a little tableau: a happy family licking ice creams; entangled lovers; an old lady and a yapping terrier; a ring of surfers with their boards fanned out around them like petals in the sand; and an obese woman asleep on a towel who muttered and twitched then let out a thunderous fart that sent ripples through the puddled fat around her buttocks. She was beached below the tide line and the sea was coming in. I pictured it lifting her from the sand and floating her off to Ireland – Greetings from Perranporth!

I was looking for a place on the beach that offered small or broken waves, where I might pop up and maybe manage a turn or two. The white water zone, as it's known, is equivalent to the learner slopes on a ski mountain. Surf waves break when the depth of the water beneath them is five-sevenths of their height, whereupon most of the energy that they've carried across the ocean is dissipated in a rush of foam. Each pulse of this white water still has enough power to carry a surfer, and this is where surf schools take their students to learn how to paddle a board and get up on their feet. They set them waist-deep with their backs to the waves and show them how to hop on and stand up. Although most teach to a formula, this doesn't diminish the thrill of your first-ever ride when you go out for a lesson.

We're hardwired to expect to fall into water rather than skim across its surface, so the experience has a touch of magic to it every time, especially as it happens without apparent effort. It's qualitatively different from travelling on a boat or on a horse or in a car or in an aeroplane. There's no rowing, setting sails, opening a throttle, applying the whip, sprinting hard, or falling downhill – the wave lifts you up and rushes you along. Such is the confusion of the senses that even if you stay upright for only a dozen yards it can seem as if you'd spent an hour in another dimension.

I found a spot beyond the surf-school classes, rested my board on the sand and lay down to do some stretches. The matter of stretching before surfing divides surfers. The old school believe that a hangover is the best preparation for surfing. If your head is sore, then what better cure than to bathe it in cold water? They are of the same philosophical set as the bullfighter Gallo, who, when asked how he trained for a fight, replied that he smoked cigars: 'What do I want with exercise, Hombre? What do I want with strength? The bull takes plenty of exercise, the bull has plenty of strength!'

The waves have all the power. It's beyond human strength to fight them. Only skill will see you through.

The new school, in contrast, believe the best preliminary to be yoga: get the chakras in line and the breathing harmonious so that you will be attuned to the natural flow of the waves. There's also the athletic school whose proponents bound up and down the beach doing somersaults and star jumps before entering the sea. I followed a middle path, consisting of a handful of prone exercises, intended to loosen up my back.

After stretching, I stood up, touched my toes – to prove to myself that I still could – strapped my leash onto my ankle and waded into the sea. A leash, or leg rope, is a six-foot length of urethane cord that keeps the surfer attached to the board, so that if they fall off they can reel it back in. Although their usefulness seems self-evident, leashes encountered furious resistance when they were introduced. 'To Leash, or Not to Leash, That is the Question' asked *Surfing Magazine* in 1972, and many readers felt that leg ropes were the surfing equivalent of building a metalled road to the summit of Mount Everest, in that they cut out the miles of swimming through dangerous waters chasing lost boards, which used to be an essential part of the experience and in doing so enabled weak people to visit the same surf breaks as those who'd got to them the hard way.

As soon as the water was waist deep, I slipped onto my board and started paddling. I was using my oldest board, which had been shaped in Australia in 2005 by Bass, the brother of a friend, as a hybrid between the longer boards that beginners use and the short ones favoured by intermediates and beyond. It was a striking shade of purple when wet, with a capital 'B' three-quarters of the way up its face, which served as both a brand and a marker.

Paddling a surfboard requires skill as well as effort: you can't just flop down on your stomach and mill away with your arms. The board has to be balanced left and right, and trimmed fore and aft. Establishing lateral equilibrium is natural and most people learn very quickly that they have to lie along the centreline so as not to roll off. Trimming, however, is a learnt skill. You can feel good in the wrong position and your false confidence can lead to pain. If you lie too far back on your board, its nose will stick up and every passing wave will smack it into your face; if your weight is too far forward, you'll bury the nose and be catapulted forwards into a head-plant. Hence many surfboard shapers put a sticker at the point where your eyes should rest when lying prone, so that your centre of gravity will be in more or less the right place.

I found I had to keep shifting position as I paddled out at Perranporth. It was a surprise to find I had to pay so much attention to something I'd forgotten was an essential part of surfing. When I'd graduated a few years back from the Bass board to shorter ones which tipped far more easily, there was usually only one place you could lie on them, so it had been a matter of feel rather than aligning a logo under my chin. Now, however, I suffered a mini mid-life crisis of having to relearn what had once come naturally to me.

Once I'd bobbed and panted my way out to the point on the sea I was aiming at, I sat astride my board and glanced back at the shore. Although I was only a hundred yards from its beach towels and wind breaks, the change in perspective was so striking that I might have been looking down on the scene from the air. The sea under me was sapphire blue and the white water from each broken wave sparkled and fizzed as it rolled past. Here, I was amidst the clouds and, over there, people were stuck to the shore like limpets. I was still some distance from the real peak, which lay further out to sea and which resembled an elevated horizon or a standing tidal wave. Occasionally a surfer from that hallowed region would appear in the white water near me like a fallen angel, prostrate themselves on their board, then spin around and paddle back out west – their work lay elsewhere.

The time had come to find out if I could stand up on a wave again. Although I'd been practising the sequence on the floor at home for months, trying to sear it into the lizard portion of my brain so that when the floor started bucking, bulging and heaving, I would intuit that I had to pop-up – and land on my feet without thinking, I blew my first few tries. I was too self-conscious, behaving as if I was an altar boy performing a ritual sequence of actions, a bit part in the miracle of transubstantiation, rather than a middle-aged man trying to balance on a slab of coloured fibreglass and ride a wave into shore. Each successive attempt was increasingly inept. I fell off the back of the board, the front of the board, both sides of the board, then off the front again and the white water cartwheeled it over and cracked it against the back of my head.

I told myself to get a grip. What if someone was watching? Might they take pity and try to rescue me? The risk – and the attendant shame – of being rescued was very real: the RNLI had an RIB a hundred yards down the beach, patrolling the patch that they'd staked out as part of their quest to control swimming and board sports on every public beach in England.

The RIB turned my way, so I slid casually back onto my board and paddled out again, aiming to look as poised as possible, and when the next wall of white water rolled towards me I spun it round, pointed its nose at the shore, stroked with my arms and then snapped onto my feet as easily as I had when I'd last surfed in earnest three years before.

The fear of shame can make you brave.

I fell off shortly afterwards, but was upright just long enough to enjoy the sensation of surfing again – that magic-carpet ride that stimulates whatever parts of the brain are susceptible to pleasure and wonder. Even the falling was pleasant – like being tipsy after a long break from drinking. The sensual confusion and blurred vision under water were agreeable rather than frightening, as was the reorientation when I surfaced: the sea is blue, the land is tan, collect yourself before the next rush of foam arrives. I was sweating in my new wetsuit, which was both gratifying and irritating. It was doing its job too well and made me long for the old baggy one I'd worn at Ope Cove, which had flushed cold water all over me each time I went under.

Pop up, rinse, repeat... After an hour and a half in the white water, I wasn't making any further progress and was tired. I paddled in, wrapped my leash around my board and picked my way through the sunbathers to the Seiners Arms on the edge of the beach to meet Ness. The pub had filled up since we parted. She was hiding under a straw hat at a table on its terrace. A wedding party had arrived just after her and they were drinking deep. The adjacent tables were covered edge to edge with glasses. A photographer arrived and shepherded the newly-weds and their respective entourages of maids and ushers to the end of the terrace, where there was a vantage point, whose orientation gave it the sea and only the sea as a background. The ushers wore black two-piece suits with a purple sheen, white shirts with open collars and had lilies in their buttonholes and sunglasses pushed back on their heads. The girls were in matching buttercup-yellow pencil skirts, white stockings, pink blouses and had marigolds in their hair. Both girls and ushers were bursting out of their costumes: they were big, happy people who cared more about having a good time than looking perfect. The photographer, in contrast, was from a different tribe. Pale, skinny and jumpy, he had little control over his charges. He held a clipboard with a list of pre-arranged shots in one hand and brandished his camera in the other. The moment he'd achieved some order and was framing the happy couple holding hands, with the deep-blue ocean as a backdrop, so that it looked as if they'd married in some distant, magical place like the Maldives, a fishing boat chugged into the scene with a swarm of seagulls wheeling and fighting in its wake.

'How'd you get on?' Ness asked, all smiles. 'Did you stand up again?'

AUGUST —— Bathing at Brighton.

4
Paddling Out

August 2015

I was desperate to progress from the white water I'd ridden at Perranporth to proper waves but the only breaks I was familiar with were also in Cornwall, several hours' drive away from home, and it was summer and the roads were choked with holidaymakers aiming for the coast. The British make more than 280 million visits to the seaside every year, an average of almost five per person. They're twenty times more likely to take a trip to the coast than to the Lake District or the Highlands of Scotland, suggesting that they prefer to be near to water than amidst the striking landscapes that inspired the Romantic writers. Surveys of their motives, however, reveal that they are inspired by the mundane rather than the poetical. Over two-thirds make their visits to go for a walk, or to walk with their dogs. Only one-fifth or so actually get in the water – if only up to their ankles. Another fifth travel to the coast to eat and stare at it through their car windows.

Our present fixation with the seaside, which interfered so much with my plans to go surfing, is recent. For much of England's history, the coast was a region of dread rather than a place of recreation, the edge of an abyss inhabited by submarine monsters with a taste for human flesh. If the sea was calm she was treacherous, if stormy, a sign that God was angry with His creation. Hence few people visited it, or swam for pleasure. Even sailors either disdained swimming or were discouraged from acquiring the skill: learning to swim, it was believed, might lead to them abandoning their ships rather than fighting to save them.

Attitudes began to change in the eighteenth century, when a fashion for submersion in ponds and rivers spilled over into sea bathing. 'Cold bathes', celebrated by the Renaissance philosopher and scientist Francis Bacon ('bathing the body in cold water fosters long life') consisted of a sudden, total and preferably forced immersion in a frigid stretch of fresh water. They were adopted as a cure by the medical profession, and by 1715 cold bathing was described as 'a practise that now has an established reputation, which will last as long as water is cold.'

The shift from ponds to the sea was championed by Dr Richard Russell, an expert, for his time, in maladies of the glands, who decided that drinking salt water and/or wallowing in it could cure most ailments. It prevented pus accumulating inside the body, he claimed, and was also an effective laxative, a pint dose being 'commonly sufficient in grown persons to give three or four smart stools.' Russell was supported by other advocates of the healing powers of the sea, who likewise trumpeted its excellence. The new cure was soon picked up by the media, who further exalted its virtues so that by 1762 *The Royal Magazine* could advise its readers that after a salutary swim or two 'cripples frequently recover the use of their limbs, hysterical ladies their spirits and even the lepers are cleansed.'

Dr Russell moved his medical practice to the fishing village of Brighthelmstone, now the town of Brighton, and built a villa-cum-spa that backed directly onto the English Channel where he offered salt water treatments, both internal and external. His remedies and investment in Brighton were followed by the Prince Regent, who made fashions of them both. The future George IV took his sea bathing seriously. He was wheeled out as far as the white water in a bathing machine resembling a shed on wheels, from which he was led down a ladder into the surf. He was assisted in his ablutions by John 'Smoaker' Miles, a fisherman's son who became a minor celebrity.

The fashion for sea bathing was adopted by both sexes, each attended by their own class of professional assistants. The men, including Smoaker, were called 'duckers'; the women, led by Martha 'Old Mother' Gunn, were known as 'dippers'. Dippers also baptized children in the art and contemporary engravings show them thrusting screaming babies into the hollows of breaking waves.*

---

* Perhaps they were hard to stimulate: Dr Russell lamented the amount of opium fed to infants in his age and noted that this was certain to compromise the glands in later life.

Thanks to Russell and his spiritual heirs, I was faced with hours of congestion as a preliminary to surfing. It was no use rising at dawn and setting off for Cornwall, confident I could reach it, enjoy a full session in the water and return home in time for dinner. I had to find somewhere closer to Dorset to advance my quest. The only guide I had at the time was a pocket-sized book covering South West England, which, notwithstanding its small size and few words, claimed to be the 'ultimate surf travel tool'. Bigbury Bay, eighty miles distant, looked to be the best prospect. It was described as a 'classy' break over sandbars at the mouth of the river Avon, good for surfers of all standards, and was said to pick up swell when everywhere else nearby was flat.

I kept an eye on the weather forecasts and when they suggested small clean waves for Bigbury, I loaded up the car and set off. The half hour of fat I'd added to my schedule was soon eaten up by caravans crawling along the A35. It was slow torture: after five minutes of inching along behind an Eldis Buccaneer, I'd spot a gap in the oncoming traffic, drop a gear and roar around it, only to have to brake immediately behind a Coachman Pastiche, which was performing an eighteen-point turn across the carriageway. After twenty miles of frustration I was too weary to enjoy a little schadenfreude from the sight of a Bailey Unicorn ablaze on the hard shoulder.

Congestion worsened after I'd turned off the A35 onto a single lane A-road towards Kingsbridge. It wandered through villages, over a humpbacked bridge, through a narrow gap between a barn and a Methodist chapel, and featured pinch points where traffic was only possible in one direction at a time. But it was a racetrack in comparison with the B-road that followed, which seemed unnecessarily circuitous, doubling back on itself every half mile with as many bends and loops as a miniature Mississippi. It was edged with Devon 'hedges' – stone banks with a veneer of brambles and scrub. Some were capped with stunted trees that had grown lopsided – their foliage combed over by the prevailing wind.

The B-road was congealed with mini-convoys trying to thread through each other to and from the sea without denting themselves on the stone banks by the roadside or provoking gridlock. There was also the occasional tractor, whose drivers behaved as if they owned the place, dragging trailers full of wheat or tankers of manure between somewhere isolated and the middle of nowhere. If you're fixed on getting to the beach, agriculture is a vexation.

The mood in my section of the traffic jam was grim. I felt sorry for those travelling with young children, whose sobs and shrieks as they blamed their parents for the delay – 'You said we'd be there when we could see the sea, and we *can* see the sea so *are* we really nearly there yet?' – streamed out of open car windows.

Half an hour later I pulled into a car park in a field a mile short of Bigbury Bay. The farmer who owned the field had a makeshift barrier of hay bales that he'd shift to let vehicles in and out. The charge was three pounds, cash only, and the farmer was amusing himself by making pyramids out of coins on the table he'd set up by the gate. This time it was easier to get into my zipless wetsuit. I tucked my board under my arm and jogged barefoot to the sea.

When I reached the beach, I found that the rising tide had corralled holidaymakers onto a mound of sand, where they huddled together like a colony of seals. Tidal movements are great provokers of cognitive dissonance in visitors to the seaside. The rising tide in Tarifa, on the Atlantic coast of southern Spain, where I lived for a few years at the beginning of the millennium, was a popular spectacle amongst locals. Many of its August visitors had experienced only the feeble tides of the Mediterranean before – which are measured in centimetres rather than metres. They would set up camp on the empty sand right at the water's edge – marvelling at their luck in finding such a prime pitch unoccupied – unroll their towels, unpack their beach bags, take off their tops and hit balls at each other, altogether oblivious that the sea was creeping in. When it started to soak their belongings, they'd drag them a foot or so further up the beach, then carry on as before, or go off for a drink at a *chiringuito*. Some families lost everything. Marcos, who ran the local diving school, told me that one of the wrecks off the beach, thirty metres down, was festooned with towels and other such paraphernalia that the sea had stolen from tourists.

*

I was an hour too late for the right tide at Bigbury. When the swell is weak its surf-break only works at the bottom of the ebb and by the time I paddled out it was the middle of the flood. The small, clean waves I'd hoped to ride, as a step up from the white water at Perrenporth, had vanished. I should have remembered to look up the tide tables before I left home and felt like a fool for the oversight. For years I was ruled by the tides as much as the days of the week, as these determined when would be good times to go surfing.

Our tides are caused by a single standing wave in the Atlantic Ocean that pulses to and fro between the Americas on its western edge and Africa and Europe to the east. It has a wavelength of several thousand miles and lasts for a 12.4-hour period, which gives us a notional two high tides per day. The standing wave gets most of its energy from the gravitational pull of the moon and follows a lunar rather than a solar calendar. Since the lunar day is longer – 24.8 rather than 24 hours – the tides skip around our diaries. You have to keep an eye on them when planning to surf, since they add an extra dimension as the sea level shifts up and down. Tides have a huge range in southwest England – more than ten metres in some places, or high enough to submerge the average house. It's no use remembering that Perranporth was good at two o'clock last Saturday and arriving at the same time a week later expecting to find the same conditions. The waves may be slamming down on the shoreline instead of rolling down the beach for several hundred yards. It can seem like you're living in a fairy tale, where the magic doors to a world of pleasure open for only a couple of hours each day, then shut fast until the moon retreats to the other side of the world.

The waves off Bigbury were now just pulses in the water. I sat up on my board and looked east across the bay. I spotted a peak that was still working and paddled over. A shallow bank in the middle of the bay was tipping the waves over into foam, which rolled out a creamy patch on the sea around. There was a surfer there already, who demonstrated that there were rides to be had by standing up and skimming off left-handed. I caught one straightaway and wobbled to my feet, feeling horribly slow and clumsy. I found I was panting after very little exertion and realized adrenaline was distorting my perception and balance. The accelerated consciousness that accompanies the release of the hormone can multiply slip-ups as you correct, then overcorrect, when it would have been better to stay still. I overcorrected on every wave I tried to ride and soon had drunk as much seawater as one of Dr Russell's patients.

My pulse steadied after a number of tumbles. The waves, after all, were only waist-high. And besides, it was a lovely place to be. The view out to sea towards the late-afternoon sun was filled with silver ridges and the silhouettes of seagulls flitted to and fro across the glare. When I spun to take off, the water in front of me turned from a mirror into a green glaze and land appeared on either side. There were cliffs to my left, with jagged slabs of red stone at their bases, which looked as if they'd only recently parted company with the rock face above, and plunged into the sand behind my back while I'd been gazing the other way.

The cliffs had zigzag wooden stairways tacked on their faces that led to houses on their crests. If the bay had been filled with land rather than water it would have been attractive, but no more – a pasture between two outcrops of rock topped with mini-suburbs of holiday homes, which could be crossed at a stroll in a quarter of an hour. As part of the sea, in contrast, a fringe of the Atlantic Ocean with no other land (if you looked along a compass bearing of 215 degrees) between you and Brazil, it felt much more of an adventure.

The sea under my board was clouded with silt riding on the current. There were hot and cold spots in the flow, composed of fresh water running out of the River Avon, and incoming salt water that had picked up heat from the beach. I slipped off my board, swam under water and dug a handful of sand from the bottom which I examined after surfacing. Its grains felt as fine as silk between my fingers. Watching them trickle away, I noticed that a voice in my head had fallen silent: that nagging voice, which told me I had things to do and places to be whenever I tried to relax, that I must keep my head down at all costs and focus on my duties at work and home, which had been a useful type of paranoia that kept me disciplined through injury, surgery and recovery, had gone.

It took me a while to realize what had happened. I remembered a similar experience I'd had in London, waking up one night at four a.m. and wondering what had stirred me, until a car drove by and I recognized it was the silence: for a few seconds my part of the city had been asleep. Now, in the sea off Bigbury, I enjoyed a similar calm, albeit internal rather than external. I felt exorcized of the evil spirits of the recent past that had been chattering away unchecked. In their absence I could think clearly and I resolved to have more days like this one. Otherwise my life would be reduced to scheduled bursts of activity, of tasks and deadlines, punctuated with fretful silences.

I drifted until the cold caught up with me. Although the sea was a balmy fifteen degrees, the sun had slid behind the cliffs and the breeze was filling in. I aimed for a pinnacle of rock on the outer corner of the bay and paddled back towards Bigbury. The water below was now too deep for the swells to break and they passed as undulations – vibrations – the odd twang on the bass. Ten minutes later, my target was no closer. I took bearings on a couple of different marks on the shore, paddled hard and checked for progress: I was going backwards. If I surrendered to the current, I'd be washed half a mile inland up the river, so I changed course and went straight at the rocks to try to cross the incoming tide. It was all very sedate, yet became harder and harder work minute by minute. I put my feet down as soon as I could stand and floundered in.

The other surfer who'd been at my break was there too, a hundred yards further up the shore, also wading towards Bigbury. I followed him, alternately up to my neck in water, and tiptoeing between shards and splinters of fallen cliff that were coated in greasy algae. I had to shield my board whenever I was among the rocks. I felt as if I was carrying a giant plastic baby that would shatter into pieces if I so much as scraped it against a stone.

When I was past the point where the current turned, I jumped onto my board and paddled around the corner into a new movie, set amidst different scenery. There's a picturesque little island off the west corner of Bigbury connected to the mainland by a short causeway which is submerged at high tide. It's graced with an ancient pub – the Pilchard Inn – and an Art Deco hotel which served as the model for the mansion in Agatha Christie's novel *And Then There Were None.** The island is served by a sea tractor when the tide is high and this contraption was jerking over the causeway, resembling a skeletal bathing machine on its tall wheels, a phantom from the past, trailing a spectral wake of white water from each of its wheels. On the beach, meanwhile, some drama was occurring: people were screaming and pointing, dogs were barking and children crying. My first instinct was to look back over my shoulder for a fin and, second, to look under my board for a sneak attack. If I was quick I might get a thumb in one of the great white's eyeballs before it ripped off one of my legs...

The cause of the tumult was a lost girl, who I could see sitting on a rock, out of sight of the beach and cut off by the

---

* The island is called Burgh Island.

rising tide. The land rose vertically behind her, and below her what was left of the swell was beating against jagged stone ridges. I guess she was in her teens, dressed in jeans and a hoodie, skinny, with long blonde hair. She was staring at her feet, looking lost and blue. I shouted to her, 'Are you OK?'

She looked up – at me and then beyond. A kayaker had followed me around the point: he had a big, fat, plastic machine with a camouflage finish and an action camera on the prow. He twirled his paddle, dug left, dug right and drove in under the cliff. At a pinch, she could sit behind him, and get a lot less wet than she would on a surfboard, so I left them to it and paddled on. A last little wave carried me into knee-deep water on the beach. I was tidying up my leash when the kayaker came zooming in beside me – without the girl. He beached his craft, pulled the camera off its nose, and started scrolling through images.

I got some great shots, he told me, then dragged his kayak up the sand.

'But what about the girl?' I asked.

'I think she's just being moody,' he said. 'She'll swim back round when she calms down.'

5

Our Friends from the West

September 2015

We've had an Indian summer this month, with still air and clear skies as autumn tiptoes in. It's been the best year for apples since 2004. People leave boxes by their front gates with signs saying 'Help Yourself', and there are scarlet clusters of windfalls along the lane onto the dual carriageway. Blackberries, sloes, elderberries and cobnuts are out in the hedgerows and thickets, and the first magic mushrooms are appearing on the flanks of the hill fort nearby. The blue moon has passed; the harvest moon is approaching. The maize grown for biofuel in the fields around the farmyard is taller than a man, and foxes and townspeople are creeping into the fields at night and stealing cobs.

Indoors, the September spiders are gathering to breed. They're a large, leggy variety that march around the carpets after dark. It's a tense time of year if you live in a household of arachnophobes. They can move, according to the *Daily Express*, at speeds of up to two feet per second, and there was a shriek every time someone switched on a light and saw one scuttling away into the shadows.

In contrast to the clamour in the house, the sea around the coast was calm. Ripples lapped the beaches. I was raging with frustration. I was working mainly from home so could swap a weekday with a Sunday if the swell was good. The problem was knowing not just *where* to go – and how to read the tides – but *when* to go. If you want to be sure of finding waves when you reach the beach, you need to learn how they are made and how they might behave over their brief, if hectic lives. Swells are created by gales and storms at sea. These begin as areas of low air pressure, caused by temperature variations close to the sea surface or turbulence in the jet stream far above. High pressure rushes in to equalize, creating gales where the pressure gradient is steepest. The winds lick waves onto the surface of the sea, which grow into a mess of whitecaps, rearing and colliding in every direction. But, as they travel away from their source and towards the surf breaks, they amalgamate into slow, steady, wave trains that separate by length with the long outpacing the short. It's possible to follow them online for every step of their lives, from the chaos of creation, through their stately progress over perhaps a thousand miles of ocean, to the final suicidal frenzy as they dash themselves against the coast. In the coastal waters around the British

Isles and further offshore – in both the North Sea and the Atlantic Ocean – wave, wind and tidal buoys stream data, including wave height and direction, wind speed and direction, air pressure, air and sea temperatures, and tidal movements, over the internet in real time. Cloud radars and satellite cameras scan the sky for a hundred or so vertical miles between earth and space. There's a beautiful live wind map that shows the breezes in coloured swirls reminiscent of the aurora borealis flowing around the continents – forming giant eddies and whirlpools where the pressure drops.*

In addition to the raw data, you can also find summaries and syntheses that predict what the sea might do tomorrow. Supercomputers at the Met Office whisk through algorithms and supply the shipping forecasts that it issues four times a day. Magicseaweed.com and Surf-forecast.com offer predictions for hundreds of breaks around the UK. And then there are the local prophets. Trev Toes, the Sage of Woolacombe, gives a line or two of cryptic advice each morning on his Eyeball TV website for his local North Devon breaks; Des at Constantine Bay in Cornwall writes feelingly on his blog about the seasons and clouds as well as the condition of the swell on the beach half a mile from his door.

Any and every piece of information is welcome when trying to make an educated guess as to when and where

---

* See https://www.windy.com.

to go surfing. I'd become a weather addict within a few months of taking it up again. I bookmarked all the wave buoys between West Bay and Finisterre. I listened out on Radio 4 for force-eight-plus in Trafalgar, Biscay, Sole and Shannon, as these regions are the nurseries of the swell on this coast. I even consulted a magic ammonite, dug out of the chalk under a yew tree on Old Winchester Hill, whose stone turns olive green – the colour of blood under-water – when a northerly front approaches, promising offshore breezes.

Trying to forecast when the swells might come also awakened what remained of the superstitious in my nature. Rather than simply processing empirical information and jotting down my conclusions, I'd close my eyes and picture myself as a shaman who has emptied himself to let the weather gods possess him, and whose eyes roll and mouth foams as he rants and roars of waves to come. The role model I had in mind was the Hereditary Porpoise Caller of the High Chief Kitiona who appears in Arthur Grimble's *A Pattern of Islands*, and whose function was to summon up a pod of porpoises for dinner when ritual, or the appetite of his master, demanded that they be served. He called them in his dreams and they always appeared, whereupon the summoner arose to greet his guests, slobbering, staggering and whining 'Teirake! Teirake! Our friends from the west... They come!'

Surfing changes your perspective on what constitutes nice weather. If the swell is pumping, it doesn't matter that the sky is black and spitting hailstones. Sunshine is all very well, but waves are born in tempests and the grey skies that spin around their fringes are a small price to pay for pleasure. After all, who would prefer to sweat an afternoon away drinking cocktails on a sun lounger beside a flat, crystalline and blood-warm sea, to a rainy day and a clean, head-high swell whose water is so frigid that you could sing in a boys' choir once it had leaked into your wetsuit?

This contrarian outlook puts surfers at odds with most Britons when conversation drifts to the weather:

'What's it doing tomorrow?'

'It's shit all day. Still, hot, cloudless.'

'And the weekend?'

'Sunday's promising. The gales should have blown through by mid-afternoon and when the wind dies the sets might clean up in the rain. But Monday's going to be horrible. The BBC says a heatwave is on the way. A high is going to slip in from the continent and squat over England like a witch on a chamber pot.'

Once you've ingested enough information to make a forecast and perhaps gutted a chicken and scanned its entrails so as to be sure you've explored every option, you can try to accommodate its predictions into your professional and domestic routines: be at Newquay, for example, next Thursday afternoon between the second and third hours of the rising tide.

*

October 2015

My prayers for the Indian summer to end were answered. It was blown away by gales from the west and a good old-fashioned English autumn set in, characterized by dying daylight, mud in the lanes, fields shorn to stubble, cold days as well as cold nights, a lid of grey clouds dribbling showers and adverts on children's television puffing large, expensive toys in anticipation of Christmas, now only two months away. The swell returned with the rain and when I cast the bones they told me to go to Putsborough, on the north coast of Devon.

I loaded the car and hurried off, wishing from the instant I started that I was already at the beach, even though the landscape was attractive and the country pubs alluring along the way. The Five Horseshoes, for instance, which I passed not long after leaving the motorway, almost pleaded with me to stop. It was long and low with leaded windows, a thatched roof, a thread of smoke spinning from its chimney and a stream running through its beer garden. Ten years ago, I would have pulled over without hesitation for a pint and a fag beside the fire, as a Catholic might have paused to offer a prayer at a wayside shrine. But now I'd given up smoking and lunchtime drinking and country pubs are slipping out of our culture. The old-fashioned entertainments that they offered – skittles, marbles, sing-songs and quiz nights, and the bantering conversations they featured, which accommodated strangers and their points of view or prejudices – are no longer in demand. The average British adult spends twice as much time on eBay as in a pub. Next time I pass the Horseshoes it will have been converted into holiday lets.

After a few zigzags I joined the A361, a summer route to the seaside. Autumn was advancing rapidly and the trees along the wayside showed as many twigs as leaves in their upper boughs, the latter lying in golden heaps over their roots and fading to a faecal brown as they coagulated into mulch. As I got closer to the coast, the Styrofoam burger boxes and Coke cans, and all the other junk holidaymakers chuck out the windows when it's twenty-five degrees in the shade and they're nose to tail in traffic, proliferated along its verges, interspersed with occasional pyramids of fallen apples.

The road narrowed after Barnstaple. There were signs everywhere telling me I was in Tarka country and a number of businesses named after that most famous of English otters, including Tarka Diesels which sold used cars. I wondered if anyone under thirty who didn't live near Barnstaple knew who Tarka was or, for that matter, Lassie, Skippy, or other stars of the golden age of live animals in films and on children's television. The genre seems to have been wiped out by advances in computer animation. What child wants to see a kangaroo saying 'tsk tsk tsk' when they can have singing dinosaurs and dancing unicorns at the click of a mouse or the swipe of a finger? O tempora, o mores!

The last two miles of my journey to Putsborough were along a road barely wider than my car, which took ninety-degree turns around the edges of fields as it traversed steep inclines, and was bordered by traditional stone 'hedges' on both sides. On occasions I was forced to reverse uphill around a blind corner and pull into a passing place so that another vehicle could scrape by. No nervous driver would ever attempt it more than once. I gritted my teeth and inched round a final bend, after which the road fell away to the left and terminated in a gravelled car park. A pretty forty-something woman, bearing her knitting, emerged from a tollbooth by its barriers to collect my money. The charge was five pounds – the equivalent of a pint and a half of best bitter in the Five Horseshoes.

Who goes to the seaside on a cold, grey and drizzly Thursday morning in October? Who wants to be *on the beach*? The phrase, in the past, had negative connotations. In the Royal Navy, it was synonymous with retirement. In the 1950s and 60s, when mutually assured destruction seemed imminent, it also meant the last resort, where people might retreat to take suicide pills or inject each other with cyanide rather than suffer the agonies of radiation sickness and cobalt poisoning. According to my father, who served in the army at the time, people used to talk about it whenever he went back to Britain on leave from an overseas posting:

'Maybe one day we'll all end up on the beach.'

'Would you take the pills?'

'No. Would you?'

'I'd give them to the children, if they started turning.'

'But what if it got you first?'

'I'd walk out to sea, and keep walking.'

My Australian surfer friend Tim had a theory about the sort of people who gravitated to beaches, sometimes at great personal cost – in the sense of abandoning jobs, partners and even pets – just so as to be within sight and earshot of the sea. The urge, he said, was born of the longing to return to some ancestral land that lay across the water. One day, a boat would come to take them home.

Simon in Galicia, in contrast, thought that people like him who had to live by the sea did so because they were allergic to dust or cats. 'We're the opposite of driftwood,' he told me. 'We flow from the land to the coast.'

I'm with Tim. Every person who arrived in the British Isles after its land bridge with the continent was washed away some eight thousand years ago did so by sea. We're all migrants, haunted, perhaps, by inherited memories of other places to which we hope to return.

The sky over Putsborough Sands was grey, with black splodges where squalls raged and a pewter gleam that marked the place where the sun was hidden by the clouds. The rain was thin and pricked my eyes when I turned into the wind. There was a handful of vehicles in the car park, including a sixteen-seater minibus with a trailer attached that had passed along the road of death shortly after me. It disgorged a class of children from the local school, who were dressed in wetsuits. Pairing up like stretcher-bearers, one taking the nose of a surfboard under each arm, the other its tail, they set off in a crocodile towards the beach. 'Lucy and Vicky, no skipping!' said their teacher. They obeyed for a few steps before the line started jinking again.

I wondered where they were going to surf. Putsborough is two miles of sand, orientated north–south. There was overhead swell all the way up, with close-out sets slamming down like guillotines every hundred yards or so and throwing out successive walls of white water that charged up the sand. Although cliffs shelter the southern corner of the bay, there was sure to be a savage current there that might drag the kids all the way out to the point and then dump them on the rocks like so many rag dolls.

There were other refugees from Thursday morning on the beach. All of them, bar a woman walking a pair of huskies, who loved the wind and cold and wagged their tails and snapped their teeth in the air at every gust, were there to surf. The surfers were an eclectic mix. There were youthful couples; a bodyboarder in his forties with an artificial leg below one knee (car crash? Afghanistan?); a middle-aged dad teaching his teenaged daughter to surf; and various young men with grim faces, pointing their boards like swords out towards the waves. I suited up, performed my stretches, waded out, waited in chest-deep water, then paddled as hard as I could. I timed my dash out to coincide with a lull. The sets were widely spaced: a series of waves would roll in and blast out white water, then the sea would relax. I got past the beginners and was only maybe forty yards short of the peak when another set appeared. I tried to duck dive, but was too late: the first wave fell on my head, spun me over and washed me right back into the shallows.

As I collected myself, a middle-aged surfer – lanky, with thinning grey hair plastered down one side of his face – paddled out and seemed to slither through the white water. When a wall approached, he pushed down on his board, tipped under it, then reappeared on the other side and continued paddling. I did my best to copy him on my next attempt to get out to the break, and failed again. By then I was in a patch of white water where I had to paddle continuously to hold my position. If I stopped for an instant I was swept sideways by the current or backwards by the next broken wave. However hard I tried to force a way out, the sea pushed back harder. Until I learned how to duck dive again, I'd be mere flotsam. Rather than waste my journey, I stayed on for another hour at Putsborough, practising my pop-ups in the white water, not far down the beach from the school children having their surfing lesson.

I went home in a bubble of disappointment. I'd seemed to be making such good progress at Perranporth and then Bigbury, and had imagined that I'd spend my afternoon at Putsborough dropping into head-high waves and sliding along their faces, rather than skulking around the white water with beginners. I'd forgotten the importance of duck diving – the technique surfers use to get through broken waves to the peak that they want to ride – and had suffered for my amnesia. You can't fly over the white water, you have to go through it, or under it. If you're on a shortboard, the technique, on paper, is simple: paddle at the wave as hard as you can, sink the nose of the board with your hands, and its tail with one knee, then kick up the other leg and aim down at the sea bed, just before the foam wall exploding towards you strikes. If the dive works, the wall will wash over you and you'll come up the other side in more or less the same place as you dived.

In an ideal world, one should practise duck dives all the time – wherever there's enough water: paddle out when the sea is flat, or on a lake, swimming pool, or pond, and sear the three-step manoeuvre into your subconscious. You can't rehearse duck dives on your bedroom floor like pop ups, as you'd need to travel through the horizontal and back again to get a sense of the vertical motion involved. There's also an instant of stillness that has to be mastered: be calm as you pass between air and water, from one medium to another. Unlike pop ups, YouTube is not much help in offering a visual guide to the manoeuvre: instead of straight-talking Australians and South Africans laying down training regimes and springing off their bellies onto their toes like goblins on speed, the most-viewed how-to-do-the-perfect-duck-dive videos feature surfer girls in bikinis, perhaps to show the learner the correct positioning of the legs and buttocks when sliding under a wave, which a wetsuit would hide. I find these distracting rather than educational, although I suppose YouTube is only capitalism at work – the popular flourish, the unwanted fade – and it would be an error to expect searches for enlightenment to outnumber those for bare legs.

6
Taking Off

November 2015

I needed more board time and less road time if I was to advance my quest. Although there were rumours of surf breaks near me in Dorset, the county is considered to be something of a desert when it comes to decent waves. No one has bothered to write a guide to it and the now-defunct artificial reef off Bournemouth was its only well-known break in my pre-hip-op days. This consisted of a row of giant sandbags that had been positioned on the seabed a hundred yards offshore in the hope that it would roll the winter swells into tubes. In the event, it tripped them over and created violent close-outs rather than the hollow paragons the town council had envisaged. To try to surf the new reef when the sea was high would have been an exercise in futility – unless you wished to test your neck against it. It lingered as an eyesore for a year or two, a boil on the swell and a testament to the vanity of Bournemouth's local politicians, who'd presumed they could rule the waves via the maritime equivalent of a traffic-management plan. In 2011, a boat ripped a hole in it with its propeller and storms tore the breach apart. Its builders went bankrupt trying to fix the mess and its sunken remains have since been rebranded a 'coastal activity park' that might also be of interest to scuba divers and sea anglers.

This sad and fruitless experiment reminded me that the key to where there might be surf lay under the sea. The science of bathymetry – or the study of the arrangement of the land beneath the waves – can be as useful to surfers as meteorology. I bought a nautical chart covering Dorset's coast and scanned it for places where the seabed showed promise. Although swells break in shallow water, they start feeling the bottom of the sea when it's relatively deep, and this influences how they will behave in the surf zone. Refraction from contact with the seabed can alter their size and speed. At Nazaré on the west-central coast of Portugal, for instance, where the tallest waves ever ridden appear, a submarine canyon, hundreds of kilometres long and thousands of metres deep at its mouth, funnels giant swells from Atlantic storms right up to the coast.* There's a similar, if smaller, rift leading to the beaches of Hossegor in southwest France, which are also famed for their heavy, hollow waves. In the absence of subsea canyons, sudden transitions from deep to shallow water such as reefs and

---

* The current world record of the tallest wave ever ridden, at 78 feet, was set here by American surfer Garrett McNamara in 2011.

sandbars make for the best breaks, especially if they occur on curved or horseshoe-shaped sections of coastline, which cause lateral as well as vertical refraction, bending and priming the waves so that they break taller, faster and longer.

The bathymetry of my local waters proved uninspiring. Lyme Bay was a series of flat shelves that stretched for ten miles offshore. Although these were peppered with ship-wrecks and swarmed with scallops, lobsters and bass they promised little in the way of epic breaks. However, with the aid of a magnifying glass, I found some spots on the coast by river mouths and shoals that offered some hope. When the wave buoy in West Bay was recording two-metre swells from the southwest I set off to explore.

You could travel the world looking for love, visit exotic places famed for the beauty and uninhibited behaviour of their inhabitants, but be luckless everywhere you stayed; and then, when you got home to dull old England, find all that you were looking for and more in the eyes of a girl you'd known for years. I wanted a break that was clean and uncrowded, and I found one just fifteen minutes' drive away in Charmouth, where a tongue of sand and shingle poked out into the sea and waves were peeling along its edge when I turned up there on spec.

My excitement was tempered with realism. No surfer would describe Charmouth as the perfect break. It's a family and dog destination towards the west end of the Jurassic Coast and was beset with groups of both when I arrived.

They were busy casting or chasing sticks and poking around in the mud for fossils, hoping for something grand like an ichthyosaur – which turn up from time to time – but happy to settle for belemnite fragments and segments of ammonite rings. There were swans in the car park and a van selling drinks and snacks. A river the colour of tea wandered across the beach and disgorged into the sea. I sweated and swore my way into my wetsuit and stumbled towards the waves over the shingle ridges beside the river mouth.

I paddled out through mud-brown water towards an empty horizon the colour of molten tin with flashes of silver and smudges of lead. The arc of the sun was flattening out day by day. By December it would be rolling along the skyline like a billiard ball before dropping out of sight for sixteen hours. There was no one else in the sea. I felt very visible and very strange out there on my own. Even though I was only a silhouette to people looking outwards, I felt the weight of expectation – if anyone spotted me they might pause and wait for me to do something interesting, especially if they were bored with their pets or offspring.

The sea was opaque under my board. Its surface was littered with tufts of weed – torn off the rocks by waves, drifting sideways around the coast to fetch up and rot at the tidemark. An offshore current was running and I had to adjust position all the time to keep the beach and, indeed, England from receding. A set appeared, its crests feathering in the breeze off the land. I chose a wave and made it. I rode it all the way in even after it had broken and slipped off it just before I smacked into the beach. It was the best ride I'd had for three years.

Elation drained away very quickly when I reeled in my board by its leash and tried to wade back out into deeper water. My wave had carried me to a different part of the bay where the bottom was covered with rounded and slimy stones the size of basketballs. Whenever I tried to put my weight down on one foot, it would slip into a gap between the boulders and twist my ankle. I floundered and cursed, and felt a very public fool. In the event, my paranoia was ill-founded. No one on the beach was looking at me. Keeping calm and carrying on, they threw sticks, searched for fossils and queued for refreshments at the van in the car park. A man was playing with a collie dead ahead: the dog yapped until he threw the stick into the shingle, dashed after his prey, hunted it down, and dropped it at the man's feet with more yaps. It was a very pure example of obsession: the dog was so absorbed with the game that a thousand bitches in heat might have strolled past and he would still have kept his eyes fixed on his master while he pleaded and cajoled for one more round of fetch. His master was similarly immersed in the action: he made feints with the stick before each throw, then encouraged his pet with cries and cheers as it hunted for it amidst the stones. Perhaps whole pods of whales parade past Charmouth, spouting, breaching and slamming their flukes on the surface without any of its dog-owners noticing.

I paddled back out and caught more rides. I came in as the clouds out to sea turned pink. My hair was matted with salt and the muscles in my shoulders ached. I felt tired, but content. If I could manage a day like this every week, then it wouldn't be too long until I could surf properly again.

When I drove back to Charmouth ten days later it was a mess. I'd had my head down at work, had spent all the hours of daylight indoors and hadn't even had time to practise weather divination. The car park was full of seaweed, the waves were raging in all directions and the beach was strewn with Christmas trees that had been washed off the deck of a ship carrying them from Portugal to Southampton. The trees had been stripped of their needles and their trunks looked oddly contorted. Instead of growing straight and true through their brief, forced lives they'd corkscrewed, like the spines of battery chickens.

I learned on the radio as I drove home that the flotsam and spume came from the tail end of Storm Desmond. I wondered if the remains of a Caribbean hurricane had drifted our way, as they sometimes do in autumn, and looked up Desmond online. I found that it was the fourth named 'weather event' of the Met Office's 2015/2016 UK storm season. I was mystified by this new practice. No one ever bothered naming storms in Britain before 2015 – they were too common. If every storm that appeared in the shipping forecast were named we'd be through the alphabet in no time at all. Why anthropomorphize them? Why reduce nature in all its grandeur to a human scale and to a name, moreover, that might have unpleasant associations? I once bought a used car from a Desmond, which a friend crashed in a forest shortly afterwards, and the name made me feel angry rather than anxious.

A little digging revealed that the Met Office had decided to personify low-pressure systems to draw attention to itself. Apparently, Storm Desmond is far more engaging to the average mind than 'Low 958 Sole moving North East, expected Fastnet soon'. People will pay more attention to meteorologists if they talk about characters rather than tightly banded isobars. While the desire to name storms is indicative of infantile minds, unable to believe what science teaches them about meteorology, wishing for magical explanations instead of beautiful truths – vengeful Desmonds rather than the enchanting offspring of a dynamic system with many variables – it may derive from political motives rather than emotional failings. The naming frenzy of October and November coincided with the UN Climate Change Conference in Paris. The rush was on to prove that humanity was destroying the planet at an accelerating rate, hence the need to unearth examples of extreme weather and turn business as usual into a pending apocalypse.

I returned to Charmouth the day after Desmond had expired. The wind had fallen off and messy, intermittent sets of waves were churning up the shingle. The sea was brown beneath the whitecaps, the sky overhead grey. I reasoned with myself that the swell itself was not much worse than it had been on my last surf in the same place:

some sets were waist-high and the best of them would give a thirty-yard ride. Even with the wind chill, the air wouldn't feel colder than freezing, and the water temperature was pushing eleven degrees. Although the sea looked like toxic sludge, I told myself its colour came from run-off – plain old Dorset soil washed into the rivers by the rain – and there hadn't been enough of that to flood the sewers so that they had to be diverted into the sea. Most of the detritus from yesterday's storm had been beached already so I'd only have to dodge the odd dead seal or slab of ply off a broken boat. But even though my head said maybe, my heart said no.

As I stared at the sea, urging myself to change into my wetsuit and paddle out, Lyme Regis, visible a mile or so up the coast, caught my eye. Will, my stepson, also a surfer, had told me that it had a peak. He'd been working for a roofer over there and sent me a photo of it from his vantage point among its chimneys. I found the message and the picture on my phone and looked it over once again. The shot was blurred, but that doesn't always matter with images of a surfing spot, as the patterns of white water left by breaking waves tell if they peel or close out. Fan shapes and elongated triangles are best, and there were triangles in his snap. I drove over there right away.

As I barrelled down the hill towards Lyme Regis, I saw potential peaks all over the sea in front of it and was so distracted that I nearly rammed a bus at a bottleneck in the local traffic-calming scheme. The town is huddled inside a hook in the land, which both shelters it from the prevailing south-westerly winds and calms the swell when it's coming from the same direction. Although the sea was as brown as it had been in Charmouth, the waves were smaller and the sets were clean. I parked right by the shore, at the eastern end of Marine Parade, which curves round the edge of the sand-and-shingle beach. The parade is fringed with coloured houses, each one different from its neighbour: thatched Victorian gingerbread in pink stucco rub shoulders with austere, stone-built Lutyens. Marine Parade terminates in the Cobb, a small walled harbour, with a banner saying 'Dead Slow' on its eastern pier, and a few small fishing boats inside. Both the Cobb and the parade had the usual coastal traffic of dog walkers and chip eaters. If aliens were to arrive by sea and make first contact with us via a seaside resort, they might mistake the dogs for the master species and offer them sticks and us chips as tokens of friendship – if they come in peace...

I stripped off, wrestled naked into my wetsuit in front of a busload of pensioners, waxed my board and skidded down the shingle to the water. There was a left-hand wave about a hundred yards out. A couple of duck dives, a few minutes' paddle, and I was there. The sea was chocolate in colour and opaque. I slid off my board and swam down to find out if the waves were breaking over stones or sand, and my arms and face were tickled by waving strands of bladderwrack that streamed up off a rock reef. But it was deep and even – no protruding boulders that might trip me onto their faces and eat my board. When I surfaced and wiped salt water out of my eyes, the clouds overhead split open, revealing a band of indigo sky as deeply and profoundly blue as the air above the Himalayas. A little December sunlight shone through this aperture, picking out the houses along Marine Parade. All were studded with balconies and sea-view windows and – viewed from out in the surf – their variety of design and colour, and reflective panels of glass, made them look like cartoon monsters with shining eyes and slotted mouths. The odd mobility scooter on the parade itself complimented the vision – it was as if the monsters had toys.

The swell, meanwhile, was small and steep, so that there was a brief sensation of falling each time I popped up on a wave. As waves grow in size the transition from horizontal to vertical – from lying flat on your stomach and pointing at the shore, to standing upright and pointing at the seabed as you take off – becomes increasingly pronounced. You have to feather your take-offs – bend your knees in advance of landing to absorb the shock, and place your weight on either your back or front foot to keep the board at the correct angle to the face of the wave on the way down. Although such intricate self-control at high speeds wasn't critical at Lyme, I nonetheless managed to fall off the front of my board the first time I popped up.

After a few rides, however, I'd mastered the drop, which was the equivalent, in terms of a vertical fall, of standing on a dining room table and jumping down onto the floor. This small feat of athleticism gave me a real sense of achievement.

I smiled, and even cheered out loud whenever I got it right. I regretted my lack of inhibition when I returned to the break and had a Robinson Crusoe moment: I was not alone. Another surfer crossed my horizon on a wave and slid off its back not far away. After I'd overcome the urges to hide and to surf with more decorum, I waved at him and he waved back. We spoke in the car park later. Nick was in his forties, dressed in an old, sagging wetsuit that looked like a onesie. He told me that the reef we'd been riding was called Lucy's Ledge, after the name of a yacht that had been wrecked on it. It was studded with giant ammonites and exposed at low water.

'It's very clean,' he said. 'Nice flat rocks. Just don't dive off headfirst if you wipe out.'

Apparently, the rocks were even flatter at a nameless break that tubed once a year, right in front of the French Lieutenant's Bistro, but it was so shallow there that a big wave would suck it dry of water. It too was a no-header zone. There were several other breaks round Lyme and a band of locals who surfed whenever there was swell. The town even had a surf shop where its watermen hung out. There were so many questions I wanted to ask Nick: was it often like today? Was it better at high tide? But I didn't like to babble, lest he shunned me in the future. So I said thanks, see you out again, and started wrestling with my neoprene.

Nick, meanwhile, put a flannel dressing gown on over his wetsuit and got into his car. He drove a dented yellow Citroën – the twenty-first-century equivalent of a 2CV.

He had a range of boards on its roof rack, including a ten-foot SUP (stand-up paddleboard), which seemed to overhang the car at both ends, like the rotor blades on a helicopter. He tooted his horn as he pulled away and left me full of hope for the coming winter, when Lyme and Charmouth might come alive amidst the darkness and the cold.

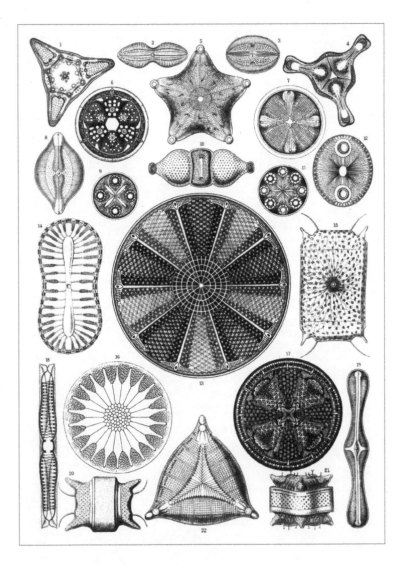

7
Green Waves

December 2015

Technically speaking, I'd been riding 'green' waves at Charmouth and Lyme – green in the sense that they hadn't already broken and become white water. Green waves can be blue, and even red as well as green in colour, and I was curious to know why our local breaks were always an uninviting brown. Although run-off from the Amazon discolours the Atlantic Ocean for hundreds of miles around its mouths, the best we have hereabouts is the River Exe. Was England dissolving under our feet and seeping out to sea? I hiked from Chideock up to Golden Cap – the highest point on Britain's south coast – to look. The water was coffee-coloured, with ash-grey patches as far out as I could see.

I decided to investigate and discovered that the colour of the sea preoccupies a surprising number of scientists. While the physics is simple – in theory a deep, clear sea should look jet-black, as no light can penetrate it beyond a depth of

200 metres and the blue we see comes from backscattering, caused by particles suspended in the water which reflect light upwards – the reality is more complicated. Sea colour is also influenced by currents both lateral and vertical – by upwellings, downwellings, the Gulf Stream and El Ninos, by relative salinity and temperature, by 'colour dissolved organic matter' such as the soil, dead plants and animals carried into it by run-off, and by the presence or absence of phytoplankton. Phytoplankton are minute organisms that 'absorb electromagnetic radiation in the red and blue parts of the visible light spectrum, but reflect greens'. They're simple, iridescent creatures under a microscope and come in a variety of shapes and sizes, like liquorice allsorts. They turn the sea a soupy pea-green or red when they concentrate to breed, die and rot, releasing toxins as they decompose.* All these factors are monitored from space by the International Ocean Colour Coordinating Group (IOCCG). The data the IOCCG gathers allows it to measure the relative health of different parts of the ocean. By their standards, Lyme Bay is fine – and proof that the chasm between science and aesthetics has yet to be bridged.

More gales with blustery, onshore winds arrived after my first surf at Lyme and the swell was blown out all over the southwest. Even Trev Toes in Woolacombe, who is usually

---

* They are also responsible, indirectly, for the unique aroma of the seashore, which is caused by the dimethyl sulphide released by bacteria when they feed on dead phytoplankton.

eager to gild his forecasts with hope, suggested that his followers turn their backs on the sea and go Christmas shopping instead.

We moved house over the same period, to a dormer bungalow in Burton Bradstock. Our new home had a sea view – a V-shaped slice of chocolate horizon, with black clouds sliding over it dragging tentacles of rain, for our arrival coincided with a gale. During the lulls between squalls, I could hear the swells detonating against the shore below. The sky cleared after dark on the night that we moved in and the Milky Way shone bright. Ness and I saw the same shooting star. But the next day the gale force winds returned and continued all week, so that I wished I couldn't see the sea. When I walked down to take a look at the beach at the bottom of the hill beneath our house, it was a hostile, raging mess, vomiting plastic bottles and other flotsam onto the sand. There was nothing to do but wait.

Patience is as important to surfing as being able to zigzag a board over glassy swells. I find it just as hard to learn, indeed I wonder if it can be a taught skill at all. I've only known one person who claimed to have acquired it as an adult, by rote. This was a beautiful Norwegian girl called Solveig ('Sun-ray'), whom I met on a Thai island and who'd just finished a two-week meditation course, in the north of the country, which – she said – had taught her patience. The course took place in a Buddhist monastery. She was given a cell, with a mat and a bowl of water, and told to walk slowly round it, to breathe in through her mouth and out through her nose, and to say, 'I feel no pain.'

She told me it was easy at first, then challenging: after four hours of non-stop circumambulation the pain was hard to deny, and after eight hours it was so excruciating that all she could say was 'fuck'. She was given some rice and left to sleep for four hours, then told to start again. Eventually, she gave up trying to measure the time remaining until her next break and lapsed into a patient trance when she had to walk.

'Did your feet hurt?' I asked.

'They bled,' she said and tucked them under her legs.

Whilst such heroic patience was beyond me, I kept a lid on my frustration with displacement activities, including mowing the lawn, which was a vivid green like the fields around our new home. Instead of fading with the rest of the landscape, as is usual in late December, these shone with new growth. Their brilliance seemed unnatural in the slanting light of a northern winter, the day before the solstice.

I managed a short surf at Charmouth in between the alternating series of flat seas and gales that had prevailed since we moved house. The sets were waist-high, clean and brown. There was a clearly defined peak off the beach, breaking both left and right. The three other surfers on the water avoided eye contact, except Nick who I'd met in Lyme, whose sagging wetsuit made him look like a farmer in overalls and gumboots, and who gave me a crazy smile as he swept by. He caught plenty of waves on his dilapidated board, which was discoloured with patches of osmosis as if it had been colonized by lichen. Its nose and tail had been mended with rough-cut squares of fibreglass that resembled sticking plasters, with hairy black strands poking out from under their edges.

I got my best ride of 2015 on a sluggish right-handed wave that had a couple of sections where I succeeded in staying on it by pumping my board, a skill I'd forgotten I possessed. I even managed some slow turns, though when I tried to kick out, I flew off backwards as if I'd been shot in the head. I rolled around underwater and blew bubbles amongst the fossils and seaweed before surfacing and reeling in my board. I was celebrating to myself when the youngest of the Charmouth crew swept by on the next wave, snaking along its face, before kicking out into the sky, dropping prone onto his board mid-air, and paddling back out in a seamless series of movements.

It can come as a surprise to see young people doing things better than you and, on this occasion, the difference between our skills seemed not just unfair but also unnatural. All the way up to middle age, I'd equated youth with inferiority: it's infantile, awkward, uncoordinated, ignorant, tactless and above all needy. It has no shame in begging, lying and crying for attention, and the moment you start to want independence, its wilful dependence becomes demeaning. But now that I'd passed over the hill, I had to accept the truth that my prior spotty, truculent, indolent self was physically superior to the current me: faster, stronger, sharper-eyed, better at metabolizing alcohol and controlling flatulence. But to admit that I was inferior to my younger self would be to acknowledge decline, which is difficult, especially if your mental aptitude continues to bloom. So how should we face up to our own decay? It's possible that there's no point in bothering. Someone else will be in command of both your mind and body when old age settles in. Rather than being the same person all your life, you're a succession of different ones – child, adolescent, adventurer, lover, parent, grandparent, senile fool. Your body changes constantly. Almost all of your cells are replaced over a seven-year cycle, so that – say – your tongue is a different organ from that which burrowed into an ice cream in 2008. Your brain too, is mostly new – its hardware is replaced throughout your life and also, perhaps, its operating system.

I hung on for one more wave at Charmouth before turning in and driving home. Storm Frank tore into the coast the next day and put an end to surfing for the year. Stranded on land, tired of pretending the hall carpet was a wave and practising pop ups on it, and raging with impatience to progress backwards in time – recover skills I'd learned and lost – I turned my back on the sea and gave in to Christmas. We celebrated with party games, fireworks, fine red wines, mounds of roasted flesh and trifle soused with sherry.

My minor triumphs of coordination during my surfs at Lyme Regis and Charmouth had been qualified by an alarming absence of lateral balance. I'd always been at least averagely nimble – could sense my centre of gravity and adjust it so that, for example, I didn't fall over backwards if I looked over my shoulder too quickly. Now, it seemed, I couldn't take balance for granted. The removal of a small portion of bone from my skeleton and its replacement with a titanium hemisphere and a matching socket, had upset the equilibrium that I'd developed since learning to walk. It was a critical defect that I had to correct.

There was no chance of working on my balance in the sea: Storm Frank was raising seven-metre waves on the beach below the house. I had to find some way to rehearse leaning-without-falling on land. The carpet bowls that came in our Christmas Party Fun Pack from Auntie Nicky set me thinking: just as this limited version of a dull game might prepare children for the real thing – or put them off bowls for sixty years – so some terrestrial activity might get me ready for the next swell. The dry ski slope in Plymouth? Tai Chi? Monocycling?

'Go skateboarding,' my brother Jamie proposed, when we spoke on the phone to wish each other merry Christmas and I outlined my problem to him. I considered his suggestion. I had skated obsessively for a few years in my early teens. I started in 1975 on rattly little boards that would jam on a pebble and throw you off, and practised moves inherited from the 'sidewalk surfing' of the 1960s. When skating progressed to wider boards, half pipes and skate parks, I fell in love with the transitory weightlessness experienced at the peak of a ramp – that split second between rising and falling when it feels you're free of gravity, which you want to enjoy again and again and again. I'd kept skating, in a dilatory manner, well into my forties, sometimes taking out a longboard to ride down hills. But I'd been wary of it after my hip operation. I didn't want to test my new joint against the pavement. But Jamie was right: the balance is the same on a skateboard as a surfboard, the rides last minutes rather than seconds, and although the penalty for falling at speed is usually more painful, the falls are less frequent and I could always wear padding.

My capacity for feeling pain, moreover, was diminishing. Although something of a taboo subject in nursing circles, where the notion that pain is 'whatever the experiencing person says it is and exists whenever she/he says it does' is gospel, pain becomes less painful as we age. Our nerves become less sensitive and we get used to it. The decline in sensation may be psychological as well as biological: there's no one to kiss you better if you stub a toe, for instance, and other adults would laugh if you burst into tears after so small an accident.

While the middle-aged may feel less pain, our sense of shame is still acute. Shortly before my operation, I'd given just the skateboard I needed now to a nephew, Ralf, to ride, wreck or neglect as he felt best. Dare I ask to borrow it back? When I next spoke to him on the phone I asked if he still skated and he told me no. He had trials for the county rugby squad and couldn't risk a breakage. My sister collected the board and brought it down at Christmas. It was a Sector 9, with a screen print of an emerald Indonesian tube on its belly. It had a convex deck built from laminated plywood and fibreglass, which flexed when you pumped it with your legs and converted vertical into forward motion. I tested it on our drive – a twenty-yard stretch of asphalt with a lawn along one border, a fence down the other and just enough gradient between doorstep and front gate to keep a football rolling very slowly. Although I was still capable – in my head – of tossing down the board, sprinting after it and leaping on, I proceeded cautiously. Memory may be a useful guide for accomplishing simple actions like tying shoelaces, but it's best not trusted for things like turning cartwheels or jumping on a moving skateboard.

Rolling slowly down the drive, outpaced by Rosy on her pink scooter adorned with Barbie stickers, blonde hair flying as she punted along – 'I'll race you, Daddy!' – I felt inflexible and frail. I'd stiffen and twitch instead of bending my knees and leaning into a turn – not that there was space for carving, in the style of Greg Weaver, the first skate icon of the 1970s, famed for striking Christ-like poses as he flowed down the hills around San Diego in California. A turn or two and I had reached the gate.

With practice I relaxed and, as soon as I was as quick as Rosy, we went together to ride the asphalt tracks between the pitches at Freshwater caravan park down the hill from our house. The gradients were as slight as our drive but the rides were longer, and we celebrated with drinks at the park's Jurassic-themed social centre. Rosy looked at the mock dinosaur heads around its bar as she sipped on her slushy and asked if they were real? I shook my head.

'None of them?'

'No.'

'What about that one?' She pointed at a fibreglass Velociraptor.

'No,' I told her, 'not enough teeth.' She nodded in agreement.

'And no feathers. Mr White says they all had feathers.'

I stared at the sea behind her, visible through the glass doors that led to the terrace and saw a line of grey on the distant horizon. Another bloody storm was on the way…

'Did dinosaurs sing like birds, Daddy?'

'I think they squawked like chickens. What did Mr White tell you?'

8
Virtual Rides

Storm Gertrude came moaning and howling and bitching outside our house that same night. She hit us in gusts – Rah, Rah, RAH! – which rattled the windows, shook the doors in their frames and ragged round under the eaves. Invisible yet audible; sensual, hysterical – she hated us all and wanted to tear the roof from over our heads. The next morning the sea was the colour of café au lait and frothing with spindrift and spume. Beaten-up trees with shattered boughs and shredded roots were beached between blocks of sandstone that had fallen from the cliffs. Some of the buoys the fishermen had re-laid over their lobster pots after Storm Frank had been ripped up and cast ashore. These coloured spheres, each trailing a frayed stretch of rope, sent Moses, our neurotic Jack Russell terrier, into a frenzy. When he spotted one he'd yap and strut and snap, and try to drag it over fields and under gates all the way home. Soon he will have no teeth. Meanwhile, the skateboard tracks at the caravan park were under a couple of feet of water and the storm surge had left cuttlefish bones in the hedgerows. A spring had popped up by our garden shed and flowed down the drive so as to make skateboarding as impossible as surfing. I feel no pain, I told myself, and holed up with my computer for some virtual surfing.

I've often wondered how an obscure pastime invented by the Polynesians, one of the most isolated cultures on earth, came to give the information revolution its principal verb. People don't pedal, hike, or drive around the internet – they surf it. Perhaps the choice was deliberate. Silicon Valley is only an hour from the Pacific coast and some of the early coders had boards. They compared the web they were building against the places they'd been and things they'd done in the real world and decided that their brainchild was more like an ocean encompassing the continents, amorphous and ever changing, than a network of superhighways or a web of forest trails. You can't find your way through it by Satnav, or by dropping white pebbles to mark the way home. Perhaps surfing was also selected for philosophical reasons: if you work in a world of perpetual upgrades, where whatever you build is soon to be outmoded, then its inherent evanescence becomes symbolic. Like each wave, you are here once, only once, not for very long, and times spent surfing – or coding in the virtual dimension – are blinks along the way between crying at your mother and being laid to rest.

Surfing has had a significant cultural impact beyond the web. The surfer is a twenty-first-century icon, as ubiquitous at present as the cowboys who ruled imaginations in the west fifty years ago, when Marlboro Man did the riding in television adverts. The fall of the cowboy and the rise of the surfer reflect a shift in values as well as changing tastes: laying barbed wire fences, pursuing vendettas and killing Native Americans and wildlife in order to put beef on the nation's tables no longer seems so innocent a form of escapism. The surfer, in contrast to his prickly and vengeful antecedents, turns his back on herds and homesteads to take on a challenge that would be utterly meaningless to a high plains drifter, in a medium where horses are useless and the only cows are dead ones, drowned and washed out to sea by floods. Rather than subduing nature and enforcing order, the surfer surrenders to nature and embraces chaos. The certainty that life is a violent struggle between good and evil is replaced by the belief that the key to happiness lies in solitary self-expression.

My virtual surfing session began with a few tubes. There are enough video clips of tube porn on YouTube to consume a hundred lifetimes: logoed mercenaries slaying dragons in Tasmania and Portugal; slow-motion action-cam sequences from soul-surfers in Western Australia; jaw-dropping drone footage of Balinese waves so clear they look like glass, with surfers firing through tubes like bullets down a gun barrel; a dredging beach break in Mexico, intercut with scenes of dogs fighting on its sands; tens of thousands of tons of translucent sapphire detonating against a coral reef in Fiji, with a man on a board tucked under its lip...

It was all very beautiful but ultimately frustrating watching people riding waves I never would, even if I were to save up enough money to fly out to Hawaii, buy the right boards, rent a house for five years on the North Shore and paddle out every day. The chances of being selected to open the bowling for England in the 2017–18 Ashes series were greater than catching a tube at a North Shore break when the waves were twenty feet tall. I could, however, buy myself a second-hand board on eBay, as my Bass seven-footer was showing signs of age, so I surfed over there and started searching. Most of the boards up for auction were non-starters: foamies for beginners; short and skinny boards for professional surfers; and even an ironing board, listed in error. There were some possibles, including a bright orange 'Bonzer', a strange retro shape that was said by its maker, in a video linked to the listing, to be useless in waves smaller than overhead. Hence it had no bidders, as most of the people buying boards on eBay were at the same level as me, were surfing the same or similar breaks, and were still tethered to reality, if only by slender cords.

I was, however, so struck by the Bonzer's colour that I added it to my watch list. The belief that brightly coloured toys stimulate the infant mind has cursed every generation since mine. Our parents duly exposed us to them and we've never lost our lust for them. It's manifested in adulthood as car-love; in cyclists' Lycra; and football strips that change every year; in the paraphernalia of adventure sports – lime green sea kayaks, scarlet Gore-Tex sailing kit, orange surfboards; these all take us back to the happy years when we were first upright and every new toy was a vivid primary hue.

There were books as well as boards for sale, including *Men and Waves: A Treasury of Surfing* (1966), whose listing had a photo from the book of one of the first ever tube rides. I zoomed in on its caption, 'SURFING – ALL IT TAKES IS TRUNKS, GUTS AND SKILL', attributed to Dr Don James, who presumably failed to notice the surfboard and the wave. I surfed over to Amazon to see if I could find it at a better price, clicked on a link in the Customers Who Bought This Item Also Bought section before checking out, and ditched it for a hardback copy of *The Magic Island* (1929), W. B. Seabrook's exposé of Voodoo and zombies in Haiti, which had been lurking on my wish list for months. If, as many people in their twenties seem to believe (perhaps from watching their elders surfing), a zombie apocalypse is imminent, it would be helpful to know – from an eyewitness – how to spot one. I finished up my virtual surf with a trip to Facebook, where I liked everything my friends were doing, however banal, and shared video clips of dancing mice and a skateboarder performing what seemed to be impossible tricks around a shopping mall after dark.

The storms took a fortnight off in early January and I had my first surf of 2016 at Charmouth on a beautiful morning, with clear skies and a faint offshore breeze. I set off from home with a song on my lips and hope in my heart, feeling that the new year promised a fresh start. All the mistakes I'd made in 2015 were bound to that year, and wouldn't carry over the change in the calendar.

When I arrived at Charmouth, the sets were small and far apart. There was only one surfer out there in the water, who fell every time he tried to take off, so gave no useful indication of whether the waves were worth paddling out for or not. I had a moment's doubt, wondering if I should resume my quest on fourth-rate rides, or wait for something better. But I was getting cold standing around in the car park, the alternative was to go home and write an operating manual for a piece of industrial machinery, and there might not be another swell for a fortnight, so I suited up.

A fossil hunter in the car park caught my eye as I set off for the sea. He had an old-fashioned A-frame rucksack on his back, a rock-hammer in one hand and a rake in the other. He was covered from head to toe in slate-grey mud, with clumps of it in his hair and beard, and ledges of slop around each boot. His natural hair colour was the same as the mud and his features – a potato nose, a knobbed chin – were also reminiscent of the terrain he'd come from. The storms had brought down a big chunk of cliff near Charmouth just after Christmas, and fossil hunters were still swarming all over it – in search of the finds that would make their reputation, or make them rich. Ichthyosaur coprolites sell for £20 each, a complete skeleton can fetch more than £100,000.

There were clumps of seaweed draped over the railings of the car park and wrapped around the concrete supports of its picnic tables, together with rushes washed out of the river. On the shingle beach just beyond, another feral pensioner was cutting up driftwood with a bow saw. Sodden cigarette packets and sachets of cat food, both with Japanese packaging, were scattered along the tideline. Interesting and sometimes valuable flotsam arrives on this coast after storms. The container ship *MSC Napoli* delivered a cargo of brand-new BMW motorbikes in crates, a builder's yard's worth of timber, golf clubs and luxury face creams to Branscombe beach when she took refuge in Lyme Bay after being holed off the Lizard in 2007. According to a local beachcomber, Branscombe resembled 'a cross between a bomb site and a car boot sale'.

Although the sun was shining, the air temperature was just above freezing and the water an invigorating eight degrees Celsius. The colder it gets, the thicker your rubber. I was wearing a winter wetsuit, a new pair of boots, gloves and a hat. I felt hot, cramped and deaf. The boots, which boasted 'Fireskin' linings and felt like a pair of carpet slippers, came from eBay, the gloves and hood from the bottom of a drawer where they'd been mouldering since April 2014. I'd forgotten how uncomfortable they were. Surfing gloves are worn several sizes too small to prevent them from ballooning with water and hindering both your paddling and your balance. They're torture to squeeze into and rack your hands into claws once they've on. Hoods, meanwhile, constrict your throat and restrict your hearing. They force you to hold your chin in the air and to keep looking left and right, like a meerkat, lest a swell steal up on you unnoticed and fall on your head.

I recovered the sense of hope that had carried me to Charmouth when I paddled out. The sun backlit the waves, shone through their crests and sparkled in the spray. A couple of other surfers came out at the same time, so that there were four of us at the break – all men – one bareheaded, two hooded and one with a hat like mine. I felt as if I was at a costume party – come in rubber – and wished I'd brought a hip flask and some cigars to pass round. Everyone looked very pleased to be there, even though the waves were undemanding – the equivalent of sledging down the hill behind the garden on a tea tray, rather than strapping on spikes and body armour and hurtling down the Cresta Run at ninety miles per hour after two fat lines of coke and a tequila slammer.

It was warmer in the water than it had been onshore, and quieter under my hood. I could hear the periodic rush-shh of a swell breaking and seagulls mewing overhead, but little else. Sometimes a shout or a bark carried from the beach but otherwise land was a dumb show of posturing and gestures. Perhaps the enforced silence made me garrulous – for the first time that I'd surfed the Dorset coast I spoke to someone else whilst actually in the water. Surfers are worse than cowboys when it comes to strangers. This break ain't big enough for both of us. More people equals fewer waves, or fools in the way, depending on whether the newcomers are proficient or incompetent. But before I'd had the chance to disgrace myself the youngest of the other surfers stopped to chat as he paddled back out after a wave. He was in his twenties, with a lanky build, big hands, fine features and a footballer's haircut whose sodden fringe kept falling over his eyes.

Where are you from, he asked, and when I told him Burton Bradstock he said wow, it had a hollow left-hand point break at mid-tide when there was a big swell with a long period from the southeast, i.e. once every other blue moon. And there was another peak half a mile down the coast at St Gabriel's Ledge. You had to walk down the cliff to it from the chapel. Perhaps he was telling me – politely – to go somewhere else.

I surfed as if I was a circus act. The toes of my new boots caught every other time I popped up and tripped me over. I made sure I fell flat, for the water was shallow and the sand on the bank by the river mouth had been carried off by the storms, leaving only stones to cushion a dive. But the waves were slow and small, so it was a pillow fight rather than bare knuckles and bruises. I was warm in all my neoprene and between sets there was the matchbox theatre on shore for entertainment. I watched a Labrador quartering the beach until, from my vantage point, it had found its focus – the spot on which to stand if you wanted everyone from one end to the other to notice you – whereupon it hunkered down, raised its tail, and quivered on its haunches. A couple raced towards it, he waving his arms above his head and stamping his feet, she scratching round under her clothes as if she had lice. By the time they reached their pet it had finished its business. It trotted off, she held out a little plastic bag towards her man, which fluttered in the breeze, and pointed at the ground: here is my love token, there is your challenge.

The tide rose, the wind changed, the swell lost its shape, and I paddled in. Instead of dancing round the car park trying to fight my way out of my wetsuit like a demented contortionist, I kept it on for the drive home. I'd bought a towelling dressing gown in regimental stripes online in the John Lewis sale, to save me the shame of stripping off in front of pensioners and their pets. It was the first such garment I'd owned since being at boarding school, where it had been part of a kit list a yard long, all to be crammed into a 'Trunk, Tin, One'; and delivered to my dormitory by the first of September, 1973.

My new dressing gown didn't see any more action for a week. The sea went flat and once again I had to exercise patience. Mine wasn't improving with practice. It's a virtue that's hard to admire, not least of all because it's unnatural – in some. While I was waiting for swell, *The Telegraph* had an article on impatient people, whom researchers in America and Singapore claimed were restless only because they were doomed to die young and could sense this. They were in a hurry because they knew they didn't have long. Apparently, their telomeres are shorter than average, but how they detect the defect is unknown.*

My telomeres were nagging me. My ability to surf was returning, work was slack, so why weren't there any waves to ride? If the weather systems wouldn't oblige, then perhaps there was some occult way to summon them? The Hawaiians are said to have believed that they could call up a swell through the power of prayer. They'd stroke the surface of the sea with *pohuehue* vines (Beach Morning Glory) and ask that a 'long raging surf' might arise from the ocean. I wondered if we had an equivalent Christian rite, or indeed a saint to call on when the sea went flat, who might intercede with God if you mentioned them in your prayers. There are numerous saints to petition for calm seas, including Wulfram of Sens and Nicholas of Myra, now better known as Santa Claus. The archangel Michael, meanwhile, has also been known to calm tempests. There are none as yet, however, to pray to for big waves who have the explicit approval of the Catholic Church. But help may be at hand: in a 2014 article in the *Catholic Herald*, Father Donald Calloway proposed that if Guido Schäffer, a trainee priest from Rio De Janeiro who had served the poor and drowned while surfing shortly before his ordination, was to be beatified, then he might represent us in heaven.

---

* Telomeres are protective sequences at the end of our chromosomes that defend them against damage and diminish with age.

Father Donald noted that neoprene had been invented by a Catholic priest, Fr Julius Nieuwland, and believed that the act of surfing was akin, with caveats, to a calling:

'Obviously, the founder of Christianity, Jesus Christ, was not a surfer. But that matters little because, as God, He is the Creator of the oceans and their waves. He is the ultimate surfer because He doesn't require a board to walk on water. In this sense, every follower of Christ is a potential surfer because it is the Christian's God who made the ocean to serve as an analogy for the eternal stoke and joy we will experience in paradise where there truly are no bad days. On the other hand, every surfer is a potential Christian because every surfer seeks something more: the next wave, the ultimate ride.'

If faith fails to call up swell, then one could turn to the dark side for the gales that cause them. It was believed, until as recently as the nineteenth century, that you could buy a wind (and with it waves) from a witch, who'd catch one for you and give it to you in a bag, or knotted into a rope if you crossed her palm with silver. I wondered if a market for supernatural weather events still existed, but couldn't find it when I searched for witches selling winds online.*

Might the answer then lie in the middle way of white magic? I once had a T-shirt of a Japanese Taiko drummer,

---

* With the exception of the Museum of Witchcraft and Magic at Boscastle in Cornwall, which offers fridge magnets for £2 that depict the act.

dressed in a headband and loincloth, squatting on a cliff top, pounding his instrument, with the legend 'Pray for Surf' printed underneath. Perhaps a swell could be summoned with a drum? I've met a lot of surfers who drummed. It seems to go with the territory, like smoking bongs. Rather than trying to relive Elvis in *Blue Hawaii,* or strumming ukuleles and singing in falsettos about Hula girls, they'd light driftwood fires in the dunes and sit in a circle trading beats, against a backdrop of sets crash-landing along the shoreline. When I first witnessed surfers drumming, it seemed to me to be a kind of sympathetic magic – if you called to the ocean in its own language, it might come. Maybe I could pick up some bongos on Gumtree.com? I tapped my fingers on my desk as I searched.

My raps were answered – possibly – by Storm Imogen, which arrived the same night and hammered the coast with unrideable waves. Imogen is here right now. Seven Stones Lightship off the western tip of Cornwall is registering fifty-two-knot winds and eleven-metre seas as I write. I've just learned from the Shipping Forecast that the Douglas Sea Scale, the brainchild of Vice Admiral Sir Percy Douglas, which – like the Beaufort scale for wind – aims to provide a descriptive as well as numerical measure of surface turbulence, goes beyond Rough, Very Rough, High, and Very High to Phenomenal.

I should have prayed for money, time and air tickets.

9
Bottom Turn

March 2016

My friend Hope dropped by one Saturday afternoon on his way through to Abbotsbury. The storms had passed, spring had arrived and daffodils had appeared in the flowerbeds round the house. It was only the third time we'd seen each other since 1981, when we'd been at school together. His son, who had been a toddler when we last met, had grown into a teenager and taken up surfing. Hope seemed grateful to be able to talk to me about it man-to-man. He appreciated that it was a physically demanding activity and so – he hoped – incompatible with smoking crack, catching AIDS from prostitutes, and other such pitfalls of red-blooded youth that might entrap his lad. He was, however, worried that it might unman him, so that he started mincing around like one of the Beach Boys, and lose his vocabulary to 'like' and 'radical' and 'you know'. I think he also wanted to inquire, discreetly, if his son was a fool to have snapped his new shortboard and had wasted his money.

'Boards break,' I said, and his shoulders relaxed.

I showed Hope my new orange Bonzer. I'd watched it on eBay ever since my virtual surf in January, and had given in and bid when the auction had an hour left to run. I'd collected it from its maker, Pete Symms, in West Sussex. Pete worked from a tin and timber shed near the shingle beach at Bracklesham, where the waves are browner and the swell less reliable by an additional logarithmic magnitude than those in Lyme Bay. His shaping trestles in the shed dripped congealed resin, like the wax on devotional candelabra in a cathedral. He was younger than he'd looked in the video on the eBay listing when he'd told people not to buy one of his Bonzers if they were going to ride it on mush. He was also wonderfully idealistic, in love with the beauty that can be created out of fibreglass, resin, pigments and foam, of making tools whose shapes are poems to motion, excite the eye and gladden the heart. Pete was sad to say goodbye to his board. If I read his mind correctly, he told me to look after her, and to try not to trash her before I could ride her properly.

I neither name nor sex my boards. I've never slain any mythical waves on any of them, nor have they featured in erotic visions, so I wondered why Pete had feminized his creation. Was he a would-be Pygmalion, hoping to make a board, or even boards, that came to life when touched the right way? Maybe it was only advance closure: he knew his creations were doomed the instant they left his hands and so he made them past lovers in his mind, which added poignancy to their pending demise.

Part of the allure of a new surfboard is the consciousness of its transience. It won't be something to test to its limits and then bequeath to a following generation, when your eyesight fades and sinews waste – or embed in a rock for some future hero to extract when they need a magic blade. Boards don't stay perfect for long if ridden hard, and all too soon a new board will be dented and mottled with dings, perhaps with a white line under the nose where it's broken off and been stuck back in place.

Each new board takes time to learn to ride and sometimes they die on you just as you're getting used to them. They snap in two on sand bars and rock reefs, or if you don't duck dive deep enough and the lip of a wave slams down on your tail. It's best not to love one too much, lest you suffer when he or she or it is lost. There will be other boards in your life – even to the end of desire. They'll come in all colours, shapes, and sizes: purple thrusters, scarlet quads, leopard-print long boards; single and double concaved, domed, scooped, with rails hard and soft; but all are doomed to perish, or waste away in garden sheds.

'Very interesting,' Hope said, pretending to be fascinated by my Bonzer.

'Hold it,' I told him and passed it over with both hands.

Hope had been an army officer before he started a picture-framing business and seized the board with a confidence that had been drilled into him at Sandhurst.

'What next?' Do you want me to stand on it?' he asked, and made as if to throw it down on the drive.

'No!'

'What, then?'

'I want you to admire its curves.'

'Which ones?' His voice had become gruff, as if he was telling his son that he'd had enough nonsense for now.

'These ones.' I ran a hand over the board's rails and through the deep single concave on its underside. Whereas an experienced surfer who'd never seen a Bonzer before might have gasped in surprise, Hope merely grunted, and changed the subject.

'How's Fi doing?' he asked. 'I'd love to see your sister again.'

The Bonzer – as a surfboard design – was a throwback to the 1970s, with five fins and a vast concave on its underside for half its wetted surface. By vast I mean three-fifths of an inch deep, as opposed to an average of perhaps quarter of an inch, for such small differences can have a large impact on performance in ways that are scarcely understood. This, in part, is because the ideal shape of the underside of a surfboard is unknown to science as well as to the craftsmen who make them. According to a shaper at Greenlight Surf Design, 'few details are known about how water actually flows along the bottom of a board, because the wetted [area] is constantly changing speed and direction in relation to the moving medium of water that makes up the wave. Meanwhile, the water in the wave itself is constantly changing speed, direction and shape, while water molecules on the surface of the wave behave differently than water below the surface,' resulting in 'a highly dynamic, variable and complex condition'. Hence a good shaper works by feel as much as by calculation, and the boards they make are instruments rather than tools, closer in spirit to a hand-made violin than a mountain bike.

I'd bought the Bonzer for its rails and fins rather than the concave in its belly. I hoped the fins would make it stable yet responsive in the fast, steep waves that I wanted to progress to riding. But before I could learn how to make it sing, I needed to nail my bottom turns. When you take off on a wave, you do so in more or less the same direction as it's breaking. After you've dropped down its face, you make a bottom turn so that you're aiming along it rather than pointing at the shore. There are conflicting schools of thought as to what kinds of break are the best for learning bottom turns, varying from big and fast to small and languid. All would agree, however, that knee-high onshore slop is worse than useless, and this was all that was available, or forecast, in southern England at the time.

But I was thrown a lifeline: an American couple were thinking of buying my house in Galicia in northern Spain. They were rich, serious people who were flying over from Texas for a week to look at mine and four other properties. Could I show them round? My house was a Spanish castle, in the old-fashioned sense of the phrase – oversized and dilapidated – that I'd bought at the peak of Spain's property bubble in 2008, with the aim of renovating it one day and raising a family in an unspoilt corner of Atlantic Europe. Then the market had crashed, I'd lost the money I'd had to do it up, and its isolation and dilapidated state made it a burden rather than the dream home I'd imagined. We managed a family visit once a year but otherwise it lay empty.

I'd been drawn to Galicia by its difference from much of the rest of Spain, which is characterized in Britain by the four Ss: Sun, Sea, Sangria and Sex; and by named stretches of coastline: the Costa Dorada, the Costa del Sol, the Costa de la Luz – the coasts of Gold, Sunshine and Light. In contrast, the only named seaboard in Galicia is the Costa da Morte – the Coast of Death – not one to appeal to pensioners aiming to eke out their retirement in the sun. The sunshine, moreover, is uncertain in Galicia, even though the province is on the same latitude as the Côte d'Azur in the South of France. Its weather forecasts seldom differ from day to day: the temperature will go up a little bit, or down a little bit, while the sky almost invariably will be *nubes y claros* – clouds and clear patches, with the clouds, more likely than not, harbouring a shower or two. Indeed, Galicia's climate is best characterized as damp. The last surviving strip of Atlantic rainforest is located in Fragas do Eume, an enchanted woodland straight out of Arthurian legend, with streams, waterfalls, moss, ferns and fungi under a canopy of fairy green.

The coastline of Galicia is beautiful and almost unspoiled. It's riven with *rías* – estuarine inlets that are often compared to Norway's fjords – and lined by rocky headlands and a hundred miles or so of white sand beaches, washed by the blue-green Atlantic Ocean. There are waves all year round, although many of the breaks are fickle rather than world class. Some compensate with ethereal backdrops. Castro de Baroña, where I first caught waves with any confidence back in 2003, has an Iron Age fort drawn in Celtic spirals of stone that juts out into its sands. On my first visit, we paddled out through mist so thick that I could hear the waves before I saw them. At the break the mist thinned, reformed, then cleared in the most dramatic fashion: I almost expected to see the arm of Galadriel rising out of the swells and pointing Excalibur at the sky. Then the white-out evaporated, the sun blazed through and the swells rolled away towards the shore. In addition to the fort and a forest, there were naked bodies jumping up and down in the white water, as Castro is a nudist beach, popular with beautiful young people from the city. There are often dolphins in the surf there. They're big, burly creatures that muscle their way through the waves but spook easily. I remember sitting astride my board while a pair came barrelling in at me. We made eye contact and they split left and right, like the Red Arrows at an aerial display, and sped beyond the edges of my vision.

I flew out to Santiago de Compostela from Stansted, spent the night there drinking deep with my old surfing friend

John, then hired a car and drove up to the house the next day. I cleaned it up for the viewing, grabbed a board from the basement and drove to Playa Esteiro, the nearest reliable break, some fifteen miles away. The road to the beach wound around cottages and vegetable patches. Brussels sprouts were in season and were surrounded with 240-volt electric fences to keep the wild boar out, their skins being too thick for anything less than mains power. A big, hungry boar will charge down a DC fence and absorb the shock. As I approached the coast, the road dipped past a tiny stone chapel dedicated to Santa Rosa surrounded by rose bushes in bloom, looped back into a pine forest, and then the view opened up on blue, blue ocean. If the swell is large at Esteiro you can see its lines and smudges of white crests just above the treeline and I caught a glimpse of one as I dropped down the last hill towards the dunes. Esteiro is something of a VIP zone on this wild coast, with elaborate shoreside facilities that are empty almost all year long. These include a children's playground, a concrete sports hall, a 1,000-seat football stadium, shower blocks and stone benches and barbeque pits scattered among the trees. I was astounded on my first visit – it was as if I'd stumbled across an abandoned city, studded with pyramids, in the middle of a jungle. There are two bars behind the beach: a smart one that serves food and has seating for a dozen people, and a wooden shack in the car park with a resident dog called Jakal, a black-and-tan mongrel who resembles a leggy Jack Russell.

The car park was empty when I pulled in, except for Jakal who was playing with a bone twice his own length – the rib of a whale that had washed up in a recent storm. The wind blew offshore through the pines. I strolled to the crest of the dunes and at each step the view grew more joyous – blue walls bristling spray, hustling in and breaking left along the beach. Esteiro is a swell magnet, whose orientation and bathymetry combine to concentrate and augment incoming waves. It faces almost due west and is enclosed in a horseshoe of low cliffs, with a view to the left of the distant pinnacles off Cabo Ortegal. To the right, the cliffs break down into islands topped with scrub and seabirds, then bare rocks – like the diminishing vertebrae of a giant skeleton – scrubbed clean by the tides.

There were two surfers in the water, tucked in close to the cliffs on the left. A set swung by and they paddled over the first wave, their boards rising almost vertically against its blue face before they dropped behind and it turned as clear as glass then white as icing sugar, and spurted rainbows of spray. One of the surfers took the next wave in the set and slid along its face with foam at his heels. I was glad they were there. If the sea had been empty I would have worried that my judgement had been furred by brown Dorset seas and drab Dorset skies, and that it held some invisible danger: a great white shark, an aggressive gang of juvenile dolphins, a newly arisen volcanic reef; or – a more likely hazard in Galicia – a shipwrecked fishing boat with a hold full of cocaine, which had come too close to shore to land its cargo and been mangled against the rocks into a bird's nest of spiked iron ribs and jagged plates.

The beach at Esteiro has singing sands that squeak when you walk on them barefoot. Their grains are so fine they work their way into your pores and clothes and you find them shimmering in the bath or at the bottom of a travel bag for months after. But it had been four years since my last visit to Esteiro and even the memory of its sands had vanished, so I enjoyed their squeaks as if for the first time when I carried my board down to the water's edge. It was an old twin-finned fish that I'd left at the house to ride on small summer waves.

I wanted to surf without boots, so I waded out a little to test the temperature of the water, but was soon running back in to pull them on. Although the sea around Galicia is usually at least fifteen degrees in March, it felt like ice. Moreover, the singing sands had prompted memories of screaming children: Esteiro is a mecca for weever fish – small, gingerish bottom dwellers with a line of venomous spines down their backs that bury themselves up to the eyeballs in the shallows, pumping an ichthyoacanthotoxin into anyone who steps on them. This causes acute, stabbing pains that can last for days and in extreme cases can result in gangrene. The antidote, which may as well be moonbeams on most surf beaches, is plenty of hot fresh water.

Esteiro is also graced with powerful rip tides, which take your legs out from under you and drag you sideways along the beach as soon as you're in thigh-deep. You forget them when you're paddling and panting and timing your next duck dive until you rub the salt out of your eyes and find you're a hundred yards from where you were aiming at, travelling quickly towards a sandbar, where swells are dropping like guillotines. Rip tides, or 'rips', are currents created by the water from broken waves, which stream out to sea from the shore when the swell is running. They're probably the most common cause of drowning on European beaches. The unwary try to swim against them, back towards land, and since rips can run at higher speeds than the fastest swimmer, they soon exhaust themselves. For surfers, however, rips offer free rides out to the peaks. Rips are easy to spot from the beach: look for gaps between breaking waves, discoloured water as they whirl sand out to sea, and surface turbulence, though this last is harder to see when the swell is high and the wind is blowing onshore.

The waves at Esteiro were bigger and more powerful than those I was accustomed to, and when my lift out to them with the rip ended, I had to duck dive with intent. If you don't get under a breaking wave you'll be sucked up by your heels, thrown forwards, then smashed down and spun around. These are sensations few people experience outside surfing. 'Going over the falls' is not something many would do for fun. Although it's sometimes compared to being trapped in a washing machine on a fast spin cycle, this is an understatement of its discomforts. A better approximation would be if the washing machine that you were spinning inside was thrown down a rocky embankment off the back of a truck. The violence is remarkable: every cubic metre of seawater weighs a ton. You get rolled and scrubbed back and forth over the seabed and if you don't let go of your board the force can dislocate your shoulders. It's best to wrap your arms around your head and play the rag doll.

Once you're out at the break, the surf at Esteiro is not quite what it seems. The beach's crescent arms concentrate and reflect some of the energy crashing into it, not always in an ideal direction. This creates wandering peaks and jacks up incoming swells with backwash, so that you can get shoved up a face as you paddle down it and drop eight feet instead of the five you expected when you took off. It's best not to look down, but rather at where you want to be on the wave so that you're in the right position if you get there and can make a bottom turn. This is easier said than done. If you were standing on land and the ground gave way under you it would be hard to ignore the empty space beneath your feet. But if you look the wrong way when you're surfing you're lost: your centre of gravity travels forwards with your head and with it your stability.

If you succeed in keeping your eyes in the forward plane and make the drop, you find yourself between two worlds going at different speeds and travelling at right angles to each other – one exploding in chaos below, the other rising up in a blue wall beside your shoulder. The view is spectacular, and now is the time to turn. You lean into the wave, slot the rail of your board into its face, and wheel round like a bird in flight. If you get it right the wave you're riding swells up alongside you, like the chest of a tenor at the opera before he opens his mouth and bursts into song. But if you turn too quickly and lose control, you'll crash into the wave, get sucked up its front and go over the falls; and if you turn too slowly, you'll miss your ride and end up sinking into the curve behind its white water.

Only a third or so of the waves in each set were rideable. The rest were destroyed by backwash, or closed out at random, folding in places where others had flowed. I tried to detect a pattern by counting them and found that the myth about the tenth wave always being larger than the previous nine is just that, as, indeed, are myths about the ninth or eighth waves having any special properties. Anyone who has ever claimed to be able to predict the quality and size of waves by counting them, from Ovid in Augustan Rome, whose *fluctus decimanus* (tenth wave) was a killer that could wipe out a fleet of Roman galleys, through Taliesin, the sixth-century Welsh bard, to whom every ninth wave was a giant: the 'Ram of Gwenhidwy, and the other waves his sheep'; to the pre-industrial lowland Scots, who tried to cure distempered cows by herding them into the surf and washing them with precisely eight waves, has been wrong. The confusion amongst superstitions is proof of their inaccuracy. Although groundswell travels in trains, which feature both big waves and little ones, there is no hard and fast law. The harmonics vary with each weather event that created them. Counting waves – if you count out loud – is a waste of breath. You have to decide whether to go or back off from what you see: choose well, and choose quickly.

I chose badly and slowly and was punished. I'd lost my balls as well as my sense of balance. On bigger waves, the only safe way out is upright, on your feet. You have to commit yourself. Think and you're done for. Hesitation counts as thinking. I dithered and fell, tried to back off the next wave and went over the falls, and after both these blunders had to fight through rolling trains of white water to return to the peak. Surfing has a rich vocabulary when it comes to wiping out, i.e. falling off your board, which you can do as easily lying down on it as when you're standing up. If you bury the nose of your board in the wave at take off, you're *pearling*, in the sense of imitating a pearl diver and travelling quickly towards the sea bed; you're a *cockroach* when you're pinned down onto whatever the wave is breaking on and can't escape, however much you may thrash your arms and legs; and you're *tombstoning* when your board is standing vertically upright at the surface while you're down below at the other end of your leash, with zero air in your lungs and doing your best not to breathe in and drown.

I managed to catch some waves and complete a few bottom turns in between wipeouts, and stayed in the water until the pinnacles to the west turned black in silhouette against the falling sun. I chatted to one of the other surfers, a Finn named Tuukka, who worked as a wolf keeper at Helsinki zoo. Between sets, I asked him what his wolves were like and he told me that they were terrified of him because he fed them. He was the alpha male. So, was he in Galicia for its wolves? No, he told me, he'd taken a sabbatical and was living the dream in a campervan behind the dunes. Waves, waves, then more waves. He'd driven down to Morocco in December and was working his way back home, chasing spring northwards. He'd already been in Andalucía and Portugal, and after Galicia was going to drift through the Asturias and *País Vasco* into France. He wasn't sure about going back to the zoo. He paused and smiled, inviting comment. I think he was about twenty-five, with fine blond hair and frank, innocent eyes. What should I say? The same as all the other surfers and travellers he'd camped amongst during his sabbatical, i.e. never go back, you've learned to live, don't give that up for a slow death in the rat race; or that his privileged existence gave him a surreal perspective on life? Would I trade places with him? Shed my years and responsibilities for living on benefits out of the back of a van, and clean waves every day?

'Maybe they want you back at the zoo,' I said.

'If they give me the tiger then maybe I will stay,' he told me, then stroked off to catch a last wave.

I stopped at the fishing village of Espasante on my way home, to stock up on food for the house. I could feel the muscles in my chest, back and arms glowing from exertion after three hours in the sea. There was still some daylight in the sky so I went for a beer at a café overlooking the bay and watched the swallows flit above the dune grass in front. When the waiter came for my order, I had an attack of nose-water. When you're spinning round after a wipeout your sinuses get pumped full of seawater, which can linger inside them for hours after you return to the shore before it streams out of your nostrils, usually at an inopportune moment. You may, for example, be leaning over your dinner, or engaged in a romantic kiss, when what seems like pints of liquid gush from your nose and saturate whatever – or whoever – is close. The emission is usually clear and free flowing but can be laced with blood clots and blobs of mucus.

'Bravo!' said the waiter, who was clearly used to surfers – indeed, with his trim figure and square shoulders looked like one himself. He clapped me on the back then set off to fetch my drink.

10
Trimming

April 2016

Spring has progressed in retrograde motion this year. It snowed over Easter in the north of England. Storm Katie blew away all the flags the holidaymakers had planted by their caravan pitches in Freshwater Bay below our house, and the River Bride flooded their playground. The wave buoy in West Bay registered some nine-metre sets; a few more thousand tons of rocks broke off the cliffs.

The swallows I saw in Espasante in Galicia have yet to arrive. The country folk in these parts used to be divided over where the birds spent their winters. The majority claimed they flew to the moon, the minority that they hid underwater between November and late March, and that clusters of them could be found amidst the weeds in rivers. None dreamed that they might migrate to Africa.

We have been compensated with more daylight. The sunset has travelled forty-five or more degrees west around the horizon since January and now drops behind the landslips above Lyme Regis at nearly eight in the evening, rather than departing under the sea at four in the afternoon. The extra hours at both ends of the day are filled with birdsong. Blackbirds and robins spit out tunes from the treetops and peck each other in the undergrowth. Their mating seasons are imminent and those without territory will spend their summers alone. The seagulls arise at dawn from the cliffs and chimney pots, and wheel and squawk at the tops of their voices, drowning out the noise of tractors on the road.

Meanwhile, there have been either no waves, or too many of the wrong sort. I found out from Facebook that Roman, an eccentric Uruguayan surfer I know from Bridport, who moved to Dorset the year before us, had given up on this coast and gone on surfari to Northumberland, where the waves were flowing but the water was a bracing six degrees. In the same post, he warned any of his friends in Bali thinking of jetting over to the northeast of England that they'd need head-to-toe neoprene, tubs of Vaseline to protect their faces, and survival suits to wrap up in the moment they returned to shore. Ben in Nova Scotia, where the temperature at Hirtles Bay was just above freezing with chunks of sea-ice in the sets, accused Roman of being a pussy in a comment on his post. On enquiry, Ben confessed to wearing a heated wetsuit and in return was labelled *maricon*.

I was hoping for some large, slow waves, so that I could consolidate the improvements to my surfing that I'd made in Galicia, and they duly appeared – unannounced and unforeseen – off Charmouth on a Sunday afternoon. They'd stolen in below the radars of all the surf forecast sites and were rolling across Lyme Bay just as I, Ness and Rosy and her friend Jenny approached the top of Golden Cap on a family outing. 'Why don't you go surfing?' asked Ness.

We were an hour's walk, at a six-year-old's pace, to the car, and there were flowers to be collected and pressed and a picnic to be eaten with imaginary fairy guests, before we could turn back down the hill for ice creams in the shack on the beach, collect some fossils, stop Roobarb chasing the swans, prise Moses away from other dogs and people's ankles, strap everyone in, and then head for home via the garden centre and the supermarket. There was no chance of getting my board and suit and going surfing before dusk.

I consoled myself with a spot of schadenfreude. The rising tide had trapped a band of fossil-hunting tourists below us at the base of the cliff, who ran around in ever smaller circles, or scrabbled at the cliffs. The wind had dropped and spun offshore and nothing quieter than a scream could reach me. The posturing was superb. Panic attacks make wonderful theatre from a distance. It's amazing how much information a distant human – who looks no bigger than your thumb – can communicate about their mental, physical and emotional states through movement alone. 'Don't get too close to the edge,' I told Rosy, when she skipped over to see what had distracted me from our picnic with the fairies.

Spring can be a melancholy season for British surfers. Although the landscape is coming back to life, the waves may be dying. It's characterized by fickle swells, whose inconstancy can seem motivated by spite, as if some Atlantic weather system had your name on its lips, and either sent waves where you couldn't catch them, or calms if you tried to go surfing. The second week of April 2016, in particular, felt like I was living through a surfer's version of the *Book of Job*.

On Monday morning at work I keyed up Des in Constantine Bay, where the swell was head-high and pumping. I invented a dentist's appointment for Tuesday and loaded the car for a trip to North Cornwall when I got home. After dropping Rosy at school the next day, I checked the webcams so as to build up an appetite for what lay ahead, which would carry me, with a growing hunger, through three dull hours in the car. The webcam streams on my computer screen weren't what I'd hoped for. It was high tide and the sea came right up to the edge of the video frame. The scene resembled a Swedish lake in a poster from the 1970s, with a few people submerged up to their waists in a liquid mirror and a dog wading out to greet them and wagging its tail. The commentary beneath mentioned occasional sets of ankle-bashers in guarded language, as if to apologize for showing such distasteful images.

On Wednesday I commuted again and the wave buoy in West Bay danced all afternoon to a two- to three-metre swell with an eleven-second period. It was visible from the road as I crested the hill above Burton Bradstock at quarter to eight that evening, with a scarlet sunset in my eyes, whose beams had been divided by clouds beneath the horizon into clearly defined rays like those on the Japanese flag.

On Thursday, when I worked from home so could have stolen out for a couple of hours and made up time later, there was a playful little wind chop that might have tubed one of Rosy's Barbie dolls had it been made to crouch.

On Friday, I checked the wave buoy website on my phone at a fuel stop on my way into work, which was showing a groundswell of one to two metres at twelve seconds that grew throughout the day and night before peaking at about 3 a.m., when it filled my bedroom with its crashes. It reached its crescendo an hour later and had fallen silent by dawn.

On Saturday morning, the skylarks were singing and the sea was glassy. The wave buoy chart looked like a seismograph after an earthquake had passed – frantic scribbles of activity, followed by a long, flat line. Trev Toes, optimist par excellence, was glum: 'Best just to cut to the chase and tell it how it is. It's a bummer I know, but a *spell of flatness* is now upon us which looks set to last well into next week.'

I mowed the lawn and took the kids to the point-to-point races at Littlewindsor. The finish line was on the lip of a hill with views of the countryside right up to the horizon in every direction: fields divided by geometric hedgerows; a Jacobean manor house set in parkland; flocks and cattle; and villages and steeples. You couldn't even smell the sea. I made some bets and won on a gelding named Faraway Star.

I hated the prospect of having to stagnate until the spell of flatness had been broken. I felt that if I could push my skills a little further I would start making strides towards my goal of catching a tube, rather than advancing in baby steps. Every improvement is rewarded when you surf. It's a virtuous circle: the more you learn about the pulses of energy that you're riding, the more of them you'll ride. You also get fitter and stronger and better at duck diving in the process and so can stay out for more time and catch more waves, and so repeat the cycle. Besides, I missed the sea. Now that I'd renewed my bonds with it, land felt hard and stale.

Just as my despair was turning into rage I found a possible solution: I clicked on an advert on Magicseaweed.com and found that the most consistent surf wave in Britain was not on its coastline, but a few miles inland and several hundred feet above sea level. Eight hours a day, seven days a week, it broke both left and right every ninety seconds. This metronomic wonder was artificial. Surf Snowdonia, according to its website, was 'the world's first inland Wavegarden lagoon open to the public with continuous waves rolling from one end to the other'. It was set in a river valley in North Wales, on the site of the former Dolgarrog aluminium smelter. The photos on its homepage showed a lozenge-shaped lagoon with azure waters and a golden band of sand around its rim. Waves drew symmetrical curves of white foam across its surface on either side of its central pier, which resembled the wings of a bird in flight.

Perhaps science – in the form of a man-made peak – was the best way to break a spell of flatness? I was suspicious: if the Wavegarden was so perfect, then why was it the only one, not just in Wales but in all the world? And the notion that I could find a constant wave went against prior experience. It was hard to believe that I might go surfing in a place where there were neither tides, nor changes in the wind, nor killer rips nor crowds to consider, which lacked both barnacles and seaweed so that you neither shredded flesh nor skidded over backwards when entering the water. There weren't any driftwood logs or dead livestock to dodge; and, finally, there was no pecking order of other surfers to negotiate: you booked slots so that, at worst, you'd have to take turns with one other person and could stand up in the shallows between rides. This seemed indecent. If man can extract what he wants from chaos, can play god and create surrogate breaks – 'Frankenwaves' – then why bother with the real sea and all its uncertainties?

I begged a weekend off from presiding over fairy picnics and headed for North Wales. According to the map app on my phone, Surf Snowdonia was a five-and-a-half-hour drive from my front door. Most of this was along the M5 and the M6, both of which were being dug up in ten-mile stretches to be remade as 'smart motorways'.

After an eternity of nose-to-tail traffic through the roadworks, I turned west onto progressively smaller and less-crowded roads. The battery on my phone died just after its app had navigated me to the edge of Conwy, ten miles short of my destination, whose medieval castle filled my windscreen. The app's voice barks out staccato commands in a range of tones that suggest it has been programmed to deal with flighty and cretinous amnesiacs. Sarcasm becomes contempt and then alarm if its GPS detects I might be about to disobey it. Its voice becomes more urgent, its orders louder and simpler:

In a hundred and fifty yards, turn left at the junction.

Turn Left Now!

TURN. LEFT.

I obeyed its last words and turned into a steep and narrow lane that passed through a stone arch in the castle's wall – designed by its thirteenth-century builders to be a killing zone – which was only just wide enough to admit the transit van charging up the hill towards me, against my right of way. I let it by, with the acrid scent of my brakes in my nose, and then pushed on inland towards the hills, destination Dolgarrog.

Although my phone was now silent, I had a couple of Post-its on the dashboard with handwritten directions for the last few miles. I'd stuck to road numbers and compass directions, for I find Welsh place names impossible to follow on road signs: they look so bizarre – Cwmystwyth? Bwlchgwyn? – and it's hard to reconcile their musical syllables when spoken with the written strings of consonants.

Tension always builds as you approach a new surf break after a long journey full of hope. Will it be small and feeble, high and mighty, an invitation to pleasure, or a promise of exertion without reward – of frustration and disappointment? Your eyes are always looking beyond the road in front, eager for a glimpse of your destination in the sea. But I was heading inland, through pastures, over humpbacked stone bridges, and the horizon was rising rather than falling away. And somewhere up the valley lay the surfing equivalent of Disneyland.

Although unmissable from the air, Surf Snowdonia was invisible from the ground until I was at its gates. I'd booked a 'glamping pod' on the western shore of its lagoon for the night, and an intermediate to advanced surfing course for the following day. The reception and hospitality areas resembled an airport lounge – a holding area for those about to take flight – with departure gates leading to the changing rooms and the water beyond. The receptionist was the picture of Morgan le Fay in Edward Burne-Jones's canvas of the legendary sorceress, whose name derives from the Irish *Murgien*, meaning 'sea-born' – after a mermaid who was rescued by monks from a loch in Ulster during the Dark Ages, and who traded her aquatic immortality for baptism and a place amongst the faithful. She snapped me back from reverie when she smiled – an expression outside the range of most Pre-Raphaelite women – and handed me a band to wear round my wrist, with a bulge where it housed a chip, giving me the power to open gates and lockers in the complex.

My glamping pod was functional rather than beautiful – a wooden box with underfloor heating, shaped to resemble an upturned boat on a beach. It was number four in a row of twelve identical lodgings, spaced at five-yard intervals along the rim of the lagoon, with AstroTurf and pub benches in between. I drank a can of cider on its porch and watched the action as the sun set. A girl in a wetsuit with long blonde hair was riding the artificial wave back and forth – and killing it. There's seldom time in the sea to appreciate the art and athleticism of a good surfer, balanced on the edge of chaos – aiming to stay, and express themselves – at the moving point in time and space where the wave is breaking. Usually you see only flashes of other people's surfs – a turn or two before you have to duck under the wave they're on and when you surface again you might get a glimpse of their back for an instant as they shoot up and slice an arc of spray into the sky. In the Wavegarden, in contrast, I could see all eighteen seconds of every ride. Although this seems a short time, it's as intense – and nearly twice as long – as the final of the hundred metres at the Olympic Games. It was also far more interesting. Whereas improvisation is the norm when surfing in the wild, where every single wave is different and you can't be sure of performing the same manoeuvre in exactly the same place on the water, let alone the same string of moves, it was possible to practise complete sequences at the Wavegarden, again and again, confident that its mechanical pulses of energy would be identical. The girl with the blonde ponytail looked like she was working out a new routine – flying up and down the face of each wave, throwing in tail slides and floaters, seeing how far she could push each manoeuvre before she wiped out. It was like watching a gymnast practising floor exercises to find out how many handsprings they needed to do to generate sufficient pace and rotation to perform a double layout with a full twist – elegantly.

It was a novelty to suit up the next morning in a heated wetroom with lockers and cubicles and piping-hot showers, rather than hopping around a gravel car park half-naked. After dressing, I strolled through the departure gate at the end of the changing room and into the surf academy, where all the staff wore wetsuits. Rick, my instructor, was tall and slim with surfer's hair, which is white blond on natural blonds, but can look like it has been badly dyed if it starts as a different colour. Some shades of brown hair, for instance, turn purple at the roots and magenta at the tips. The phenomenon is caused by the bleaching action of salt water. The only shade it doesn't affect is grey. Rick's hair was chocolate, copper and gold as it spiralled outwards from his scalp. He was Dutch and said 'schh' instead of 'ts' – 'it's' came out as 'ischh' – which made him sound like an enthusiastic drunk.

We began by deconstructing the pop-up. Rick demonstrated it to me at full speed, then again in slow motion: push up off your chest, back foot down, front foot down, and rise. He was ridiculously light on his feet, which were huge, yet didn't trip him up. He was also very smooth in his movements and I had to ask him to slow down even more.

'Pretend you're in a cartoon,' I said.

'Like Mickey Mouschh?'

'Like Spiderman.'

'*Spiderman*sch a movie.'

'Like Andy Capp then. Frame by frame.'

'I fall over if I move too schlow.' He tried and did just that. He laughed.

The secret to a good pop-up is being half my age.

But Rick was pleased with my efforts. Apparently, some of his students couldn't ascend from their bellies at all, and lay around rolling their eyes and puffing like beached walruses. He picked me a foam longboard from the rack and we marched out to play in the wave garden.

Surf Snowdonia makes its swell with a 'wavefoil' – a computer-controlled steel plough, which is dragged to and fro along the middle of its lagoon by cables and pulleys. The waves created by the plough break in accordance with concrete ridges on the bed of the lagoon, and feed three zones for advanced, intermediate and beginner surfers. Riders are protected from the plough and its whirring steel cables by chain-link fencing. My mission was to master the 'intermediate wave', which was described on Surf Snowdonia's website as a 'waist-high green wave', and in the process to learn, as Rick put it, how to 'trim my schtick'.

'Itsch easchy,' he said, and outlined the plan of attack:

When I popped up I was to press down on my left hand and shift my weight onto my heels, look back over my shoulder, then push down with my front foot as the wave turned. And to remember to jump off and cover my head with my hands when I reached the end of the ride a few seconds later. Rick, meanwhile, would skateboard round the rim of the lagoon and film me on his iPad. He pointed out where to wait in the water: ten yards in from a sign on the chain-link fence around the wavefoil. I was to stand on tiptoes on the edge of the reef, start paddling when the cables ran, angle my board so that it was perpendicular to the wave, and perform the prescribed sequence of actions as soon as I was upright.

The lagoon is fed by rainwater from the adjacent hydro-electric plant. It was the colour of tea and filled with little brown spots of mucus. It felt very different from the sea: I was far less buoyant, and its taste was sweet and sour on the tongue rather than cauterising and salty. I paddled out a few strokes towards the central pier and took up my station. Time stretches when you're waiting for the starting gun and your senses are tingling with anticipation. Birds slow down in flight. You can count ten seconds and only two have passed. The suspense was magnified by the relative quietness of the lagoon. When a head-high swell is breaking that close in the sea it sounds like you're trapped in a dustbin with someone pounding on its lid. At Dolgarrog there were lambs bleating in the fields and robins singing from the trees.

The spell was broken when the cables on the wavefoil began to whirr. I looked over my shoulder and saw a bulge emerge in the water around its shaft. I thought at once of

Jaws when the great white shark, fin erect, comes steaming in towards whatever it's about to maul. As white water rushed around my ears I angled and paddled and pressed, then popped up at what seemed so rickety a pace that the wave would have finished before I found my feet. Then I was upright with a knee-high wall to my right that I tucked into and shot along – towards ankle-deep water at the edge of the pond, where I had to flip the board side-on to stop running ashore, and ended up quivering on my back with my legs in the air and a nose-full of Welsh mountain run-off.

Rick gave me a thumbs-up and waved me out the water. We hunched over his iPad and he showed me me. The video was an interesting demonstration of the difference between perception and truth when the adrenaline is flowing: while it had seemed to take forever to get to my feet it looked instantaneous on a screen in real time: blink and you'd have missed it.

Rick paused the action and drew a green arrow across the screen with his finger, showing me where I should have gone, then let play resume as I flew off in the opposite direction and ended up thrashing and twitching in the shallows, as if fighting an invisible snake.

'Thisch isch left,' Rick said, showing me one hand, 'and thisch isch right,' holding up the other.

I stood tall and fell on the following wave, went the right way on the one after and fell again because I leant backwards too far too fast. Triumph alternated with disaster for the rest of the session. If I caught a wave properly my confidence rocketed and I'd pop up into a forward roll off the end of the board on the next. But I was learning, most importantly, about the proper way to travel sideways along a wave – even when I went the wrong way.

My next task was to master the 'advanced wave', the Wavegarden's head-high centrepiece that broke down the middle of the lagoon. I'd brought the Bonzer, but Rick took one look at it and told me to stick to the foam board I'd been thrashing about on for the last hour. I needed to learn how to balance it fore and aft – step forward to accelerate, step backwards to brake or turn. It was better to perfect this technique – called trimming – on a longer board, which was more forgiving and would damp down errors rather than magnifying them.

The board was too big to fit under my arm comfortably, so I balanced it on my head and followed Rick back to the lagoon. He told me that this time, I was to wait right by the chain-link fence around the lagoon's central pier. The take off on the advanced wave was steeper and quicker and I was to start paddling the instant I heard the cables running. Right-hand down as I popped up, then transfer my weight onto my toes straight away, then sit a little on my heels and let the rail hold me in place on the wave. Jump off backwards if I made it to the end so as not to hit a learner in the beginners' zone. Perform the same sequence in reverse when the wave plough travelled in the opposite direction. The challenge was to try to think about what I was doing when on the wave rather than just reacting then over-compensating.

'Train the brain,' Rick said. He tapped his head and pointed at mine.

'Right,' I said.

I got up first try and for an instant felt that I ruled all creation. There wasn't time to develop the fantasy in any detail beyond a fleeting conviction of omnipotence and the desire to do good in this most beautiful of worlds. By now, of course, I was standing bolt upright, my arms reaching towards the sky, and when I fell I landed on my face with my eyes wide open. Fresh water stings the eyeballs in a different way from salt. It feels like they're being pricked with needles rather than scoured with wire. On this occasion, the needles dug under the lens in my right eye and I wondered if this was what it felt like when you detached a retina. Would I be able to see properly when I surfaced? I kept it closed and paddled back into position for the next ride. Cognitive dissonance has its uses. Sometimes reason must give way to pleasure and partial blindness – or not – could wait for a wave or two.

Or ten. Even though the wave was always the same I couldn't read it, and became frustrated that I couldn't anticipate the predictable. It was like being on a production line in a factory and getting tossed off the conveyor belt at random: Pass. Fail. Pass. Fail. Fail. But the passes made it worthwhile: I'd opened both eyes and the thrill of being swept along aloft on a moving wall of water kept me trying until my muscles burned.

I was sharing the 'advanced wave' with one other surfer. He had a full suit of neoprene, boots, gloves and a curious cap. His profile looked familiar. I ransacked my memory for its match, and up swam a portrait of a Plantagenet King – same hawk nose and gritted jaw. He rode an identical foam board to me, which he slowly but surely mastered, and a beatific smile spread over his face. He was wrapped up in his own space – bewitched even. Each next ride was better than the last and every new wave a journey of discovery.

When I came in at the end of the session Rick laughed at me and said 'Your eye isch bleeding.'

'Badly?'

'Maybe Rick imagined it.' An instructress in a wetsuit appeared by his shoulder, smiled at me, and guided him away.

My right eye was still smarting when I went to change and I checked it in the mirror after I'd showered. There was a patch of scarlet under the iris – Rick had been right, though I took his remark as a compliment rather than an indiscretion. He'd treated me as a fellow surfer and expected me to make light of any injury, whether grave or trivial, rather than as a customer, a stranger who'd come to pay and play in the Wavegarden.

11
Rail Riding

May 2016

Spring has exploded into summer. The world has closed in around our house as surging vegetation blots out chunks of the view. The slice of sea across the southern horizon has been reduced to a fuzzy 'V' between two trees. The sea itself is flat. People gabble about the sunshine – and offer it their flesh. A shantytown of caravans and camper vans has sprung up on the flood plain behind Freshwater Beach and the smoke from a hundred campfires mingles in the air above.

The Met Office took advantage of the heatwave to predict a 'barbecue summer' for 2016. Its long-term forecasts are fantastically inaccurate, in the sense that they underperform the law of averages so badly as to suggest wishful thinking. My heart leapt when I heard the news on the radio: I was driving to Charmouth and feeling so down about the prospects of finding any swell that I had a fishing rod as well as a surfboard in the back of the car. I cheered out loud after this token of hope for the forthcoming months was announced.

Most years, the swell drops off round Britain during summer. A high-pressure system settles over the Azores archipelago mid-Atlantic and deflects the turbulent, wave-creating lows north. If, however, the Azores High is feeble, the lows march in and wasted hurricanes track back from the Caribbean to flood us with rain. The Met Office has a nought-from-four success rate with its twenty-first-century 'barbecue summers'. Nature has elected to throw mud in the eyes of its meteorologists every time they have suggested one is on the way and has sent flash floods, overcast skies, hailstorms and even the odd twister as punishments for their presumption. Their would-be halcyons are typified by washed-out Test matches, mud knee-deep at Glastonbury and havoc on the stock exchange, as retailers have to switch from bikinis to raincoats and take the hit on their bottom lines.

And waves.

I turned the car around and checked the long-range surf forecasts when I got home. Trev in Woolacombe was all love as he prophesied swell from Tuesday onwards, with the wind dying and veering offshore on Thursday, when conditions would be perfect. Throw a sickie at work, tell your partner you'll be away on business and get yourself down to the beach for the late-afternoon tidal push. There was swell expected on the south coast of Devon too. Magicseaweed. com promised energetic five-foot waves with a cross/offshore wind for Bantham Beach.

That Thursday, I dropped Rosy at school and headed west. The curse of the 'barbecue summer' had exceeded my expectations. There had been floods and lightning strikes up and down the country. Ravensworth in Yorkshire, Dunstable in Bedfordshire, and Wallington and parts of Croydon in the London suburbs were under water, and there was swell all around the coast.

I drove to Bantham, across the bay from Bigbury where I'd been washed up the Avon last autumn. The final few miles of the route were down a similarly narrow lane, also edged with stone hedges, which had a couple of feet of newly grown nettles poking out from them that constricted the roadway even further. The car park at its terminus was in fields above the headland on a private estate. Entry was via a barrier manned by a grim-faced and red-nosed retainer, who scowled through his beard and said, 'That's six pounds.'

I unclipped my seat belt so I could fetch the money from my pocket.

'I think it's clearing up,' I said, and pointed at a small patch of blue in the sky on the horizon.

'That's six pounds,' he repeated, as if these were the only words he knew. I gave him a five-pound note and a one-pound coin, which he made a show of counting before issuing me with a ticket.

The fields that constituted the car park were greasy with mud and there were puddles in the ruts across them. The sky, however, *was* clearing. The rent of blue in the clouds had become an azure chasm. I parked as close as I could to the sea and walked down to the beach to take a look. One glance at the water told me all I needed to know: shoulder-high waves, breaking both left and right from the peak. I wanted to stretch my legs before I suited up, so I strolled along the tidemark for a few minutes. I kept my eyes down, scanning the sand at my feet, in the hope of spotting some relic of Bantham *antiquior*. Jane had told me she'd found a piece of ancient pottery in the sand and that her friend Sam had picked up a Celtic amulet among the rocks at low tide. Bantham, she said, was one of a ring of lost settlements around the coast of southwest England, all sited astride powerful ley lines that radiated from Glastonbury Tor. It was a magnet for relics, she added, and opened her eyes wide, as if the knowledge of such powers was a kind of enlightenment. I looked it up online.

While archaeologists' reports on Bantham didn't mention mystic bands of power underground, it turned out to have plenty of past. The Bantham Surf Life-Saving Club in the eastern corner of the beach was built over what might have been a Roman tavern. There are also the traces of a sizeable Roman village beneath the car park. This, like so many other coastal settlements, was abandoned during the Dark Ages and vanished under the dunes. The Anglo-Saxons gave it its present name. *Ban-* means 'bone', and *-ham* denotes 'land hemmed in by water' – in other words it was a graveyard on a promontory. There's evidence to suggest that it was inhabited again during medieval times, as human remains from that era have been found jumbled together with Roman skeletons, like driftwood after a storm. The later burials may also have been the mass graves of shipwrecked sailors, or the victims of the pirates who nested at Burgh Island across the bay. There seem to have been so many burials at Bantham that each fresh grave was dug into an existing one. Most of the bones were removed in the eighteenth century after a storm rearranged the dunes and uncovered mounds of them, which local landowners carted away to grind up as fertilizer for their turnips.

I returned to my car and changed, then carried my board to the beach and lay down at the water's edge to stretch. I spotted a tooth sticking out of the sand beside my head, inches from my nose. It was ridged and jagged and pitted and its enamel was stained tobacco-brown. Could it be human? Was it a relic of the jaws and skulls that had been removed to nourish tubers? The idea of owning a Roman tooth was exciting. I could keep it safe under my wetsuit while I went surfing, then have it mounted in silver and give it to Jane for Christmas. I dug it up when I finished stretching. It came from a sheep.

A picture-perfect rip current ran parallel to the rocks at the east side of Bantham, whirling seaweed and suspended sand back out to sea. I rode it on my belly, paddling to control where I was going rather than for motive power. I made a couple of duck dives, dodged a few boulders, and sat up once I got out the back. There were lots of people at the break, all friendly, each making eye contact and flashing smiles – as if to say – aren't we lucky to be here?

The waves were slow. They wobbled like belly fat before they broke. Their tops would split like overstretched skin and dribble foam, and the remainder would flop over, sag and rupture, spilling a mess of spume. They were also hard to catch. I had to windmill my arms through the water then shove my board down their faces to get planing. Of the other surfers, the longboarders were having the best of it. They glided over flat sections, burrowed through the patches of white water and rode all the way into the beach. We shortboarders however had to pump like fury just to stay with the waves for more than a few seconds.

Pumping is bouncing up and down on the balls of your feet on your board, flexing your knees to convert vertical movement into horizontal motion. When you're good at it it's all in the legs; when you're bad you need your arms too and it looks ridiculous, as if you were a child flapping your elbows like wings and pretending to fly. I waved my arms up and down like Herbert von Karajan leading the Berlin Philharmonic through Beethoven's *Fifth Symphony*, and flexed my legs out of time with both arms and waves, but managed, nonetheless, to transform some of this frantic jiggling into forward motion. As ever, I was absorbed in the moment – fighting for control, losing it, winning it back a millisecond before wipeout, then teetering on the precipice again the next instant. By fluke, rather than concentration and miracles of co-ordination, I had one great ride on a shoulder-high wave that carried me along with such ease that I had time to relax, look up from my feet, and watch the wave rise up beside me as I scooted along its face. The sense of satisfaction when I flopped off at the end was intense. It ignited my hope and rather than taking the easy way back to the break by riding the rip, I duck dived my way there through the white water. When I sat up to rest, the sky to seaward had cleared entirely and sunlight gilded the ocean. Bantham, meanwhile, was still under black-bellied clouds which discharged lightning bolts into the car park – no doubt charging its ley lines.

It was my best wave of the day. On the next one I dropped in on a longboarder, whose deck was glassed to look as if it had been veneered in alternating strips of renewable bamboo and teak. He seemed to appear from behind the wave, as if he'd been lurking in its trough, and claimed right of way just after I'd got to my feet so that I had to grab my rail and dig back into its face – and exchange another magic carpet ride for a short subaqueous thrashing.

Although there are no formal rules to surfing – in theory you're free to catch any wave you can – there's a simple etiquette, observed all round the world, as to when to give way to another surfer on the same wave, as follows: the person who takes off closest to its shoulder has right of way, and if you've dropped in on someone else's ride, you have a moral duty to bail out. At crowded or difficult breaks this simple precedence is enforced with violence. The laid-back image of the surfer dude hides a mean streak, which emerges under the pressure of competing for waves. Some spots are famed for their 'localism', i.e. the territoriality of the local surfers, who protect their turf against visitors with a fanaticism that the Spartans would have admired. Rule breakers are punished with blows, are pulled off their boards by their leashes at dangerous points in the wave, and find their cars vandalized when they return to land. It is all very Darwinian.

There wasn't any localism on show at Bantham that day. The waves were becoming slower and were scarcely worth fighting for. I tried as hard as I could to catch them, most times with the same result: take off, lose speed, sink – still upright – into the water as the wave rolled away, paddle back and repeat. I felt caught in a loop and my mood soured – all that wasted energy for so little action. As I meditated on the transience of pleasure, another longboarder whizzed past, strutted up to the nose of his board and stuck the toes of one of his feet over its edge, 'hanging five', grinning as if he'd just entered a new dimension. His ride went on and on and on. As the wave got smaller and the shore closer, he skipped back into the centre of his board where he stood with his feet together like a soldier on parade. He hopped off just before it grounded its fin on the sand.

I was impressed. In that single ride, he'd covered more sea than I had in my previous five. He'd even found time to pose. I sat to the side of the break and compared the performance of shortboarders and longboarders. There were some good surfers on little pointed missiles who could whip the top of a wave for a turn or two, but even the bad longboarders travelled further, and sometimes faster. The disparity increased as the tide went slack and the swell dropped off. There were fewer and fewer rideable waves and since the longboarders could catch them further out, they caught almost all of them. When competing for them became pointless, I paddled in.

My surf at Bantham had been a foretaste of what was to come once the 'barbecue summer' eased up. When still air and sunny skies returned, another spell of flatness would settle over Ultima Thule. The swells would hobble in, not tall enough to menace a nervous five-year old – if they appeared at all. It would make more sense to try to catch fish rather than waves if I went to the beach.

The prospect of not being able to surf for weeks was painful. It had become part of my life once again. I felt healthier than I had been for years. My shirts were tight around the chest and shoulders as well as the waist. My face and hands were tanned above the cuff and collar lines of my wetsuit. I'd even started dropping surfer slang into my speech. If a person was happy or excited about something, I'd say they were 'stoked'; if they bounced round with energy they were 'charging'; and if dull and listless they were 'flotsam'. Sadly, the only way I could see around a period of 'hodading', i.e. going to the seaside and *not* surfing, was to become a 'logger', or longboarder.

Although surfers everywhere are brothers and sisters under the skin, they tend to belong to one of three tribes

– longboarders, shortboarders and bodyboarders. While the tribes mix freely and even mate occasionally, they have different worldviews, evident in their stereotypes of one another, and indeed themselves. Longboarders believe that they are the guardians of the spirit of surfing and that shortboarders violate waves instead of respecting them and riding them only when the time is right. Shortboarders, meanwhile, accuse loggers of retrophilia and mock their obsession with nose riding and other such arcana. Both shortboarders and longboarders agree that 'spongers', i.e. bodyboarders, are the kamikazes of the surfing world, who seek glory in oblivion and would be sitting at the back of the classroom tattooing their hands with compass points and biro ink, or banging their heads against their bedroom walls in time to AC/DC if they weren't riding sucking beach breaks and testing their ribs and collar bones against sandbars.

Switching affiliation between tribes is difficult. There are bigotries to strangle, gut-hatreds to suppress and aesthetic preferences to rearrange. Each tribe travels with a lot of baggage and you have to jettison some of the old to make space for the new. Longboarders were filed in my head alongside Morris dancers, MGB owners, real-ale fanatics and Harley Davidson riders. Although I would never have slandered them to the extent of linking them to golf, I could picture them twitching to *Kind of Blue* by Miles Davis, which was disturbing. But they'd had fun at Bantham, while we shortboarders had struggled. I knew I needed a longboard, even if I didn't want one. I had to learn to be open-minded, or at least broadminded, about longboards and stop recoiling from them as if they were imbued with evil spells, or were toxic to my kind.

Instead of reflecting on the boards themselves, I decided to grow my affection for them by getting inside the minds of their riders. I thought back to the first longboarder I'd met: Rick, who lived in the Bundageon community in New South Wales and surfed naked on a board shaped like a ten-foot long spermatozoa, with a rounded head and a skinny tail. No one else could ride it. Rick was sixty years old, and considered to be something of a tight-lipped seer. He only ever spoke to me once, after I came in over the rocks and their barnacles gouged tracks into my shin.

'They didn't bite you too bad,' he said, and smiled. He was right: the cuts bled copiously but didn't need stitching.

And then there was Bill, an avuncular and bearded Californian I got chatting to at a regatta in Tiburon. Bill told me he was heading down to Cabo in December on the Baja Ha-Ha yacht rally, and invited me to come and see his Bing spoon: he was going to lash it to the deck and do some nose riding when he got to 'Mehico'. He also told me that his favourite book of all time was *Jonathan Livingston Seagull*. Perhaps the book might provide a window into the mind of a longboarder? I hadn't read it since my teens, when people had raved about the clever blend of contemporary aerodynamic theory and timeless soul-searching that its author Richard Bach had used to fill the stream-of-consciousness of his hero-gull. I'd affected to like it because I'd been told it was a deep poetic read, and didn't dare stand against the crowd at that age. My principal memories of it were that it was inoffensive and mercifully short: *The Prophet* rather than *Watership Down*. It was time to give it a second try.

It would be an understatement to say that I was 'bummed out' when a copy arrived from Amazon. It was far smaller than I'd remembered and I'd forgotten its execrable black-and-white photos of seagulls and terns – blurred spectres with ragged feathers adrift in cloudy, grainy, gloomy skies. These images revived memories of England in the 1970s – soot, strikes, blackouts and pinched and angry faces on television and in the streets – and my heart sank.

The day it arrived the evening was clear, so I set aside my misgivings, unfolded a deck chair on the lawn, opened a beer and sat down to read. I'd finished it in half an hour, although after a very few pages the minutes dragged. I hoped its Part Two was the last and was disappointed to find a Part Three. I was distracted at its climax, when Ness fed the dogs in the garden and real-live Jonathans dropped from the chimney pots to fight over the scraps they'd left in their bowls. Was Jonathan Livingston Seagull a Platonist, a Taoist, a Nietzschean, a Fascist, or a muddle of all four ethea? What is he implying, for instance, when he tells his disciples that, 'Each of us is in truth an idea of the Great Gull, an unlimited idea of freedom... and precision flying is a step towards expressing our real nature. Everything that limits us we have to put aside'?

Fortunately, I'd also bought *Surf Craft*, a hardback catalogue from a 2015 exhibition of vintage and modern surfboards at the Mingei International Museum of San Diego, at the same time as *JLS*. I'd ordered it as a backstop on the evidence of its cover, which showed rows of boards of all shapes and sizes – like coloured sweets – hoping its beautiful photos and descriptions of surfboards past and present might help me connect to longboarding if the gull-allegory failed. In the event *Surf Craft* focused on the death of the longboard in the face of the revival of ancient Hawaiian shortboards, the application of hydrodynamics to modern creations, and the influence of skateboarding over surfing. In despair, I turned to eBay. Maybe somebody had a longboard for sale that I could love, which would leap out of the listings, like a dog springing off its mat in an animal shelter – muzzled, perhaps, but wagging its tail and radiating mute longing.

Sometimes we find our dreams incarnate in cyberspace. Google a vague phrase and score a direct hit: a corporeal version of a mental image of an object that you'd only ever imagined might exist appears for sale, complete with photos, dimensions and shipping arrangements. I found my dream non-longboard longboard in a buy-me-now posting on eBay.co.uk. It was shaped like the top half of a lollipop stick with a rounded nose and a square tail – 6'3" × 23" × 2½" – white on top, orange underneath, with two big fins. It was advertised as a 'little lady' for longboarders or a 'summer log' for shortboarders, and labelled a 'Mini Simmons', which rang a bell. I discovered a photo of its prototype in *Surf Craft*, together with a few lines on its inventor, Bob Simmons, who'd driven a stake into the heart of long-boarding back in the 1940s. Simmons built 'hydrodynamic planing hulls', surfboards so fast they took off on big waves. They were, moreover, mere diddle sticks compared to existing boards – only eight feet long and less than fifty pounds in weight. Best of all, they went as easily along the face of a wave as in front of it. Simmons's principal insight was that a surfboard is actually travelling parallel to the beach as much as going towards it, and should be shaped to reflect this. 'We are really surfing on our rails,' he explained, as it was these that generated lift from the faces of swells.

Simmons was inspired to start surfing and building his own boards after he suffered a serious injury in his teens. While cycling to build up his strength as part of his recuperation from cancer of the ankle, he was run over by a car. The accident fractured his skull, broke one of his legs and damaged his left arm so badly that it had to be wired into a set position thereafter. During his months of convalescence in hospital, Simmons met a surfer with a broken leg, who advised him to ride waves to get fit again and told stories of giant swells that had closed right over his own head while he ghosted along inside. In Simmons's words, 'According to this surfer, you're riding along in this softly lit green room and it is so quiet that if you whistle or yell, you can hear the echo!'

Simmons built his boards on sound scientific principles. He had a talent for mathematics as well as accidents. He was conversant with all the authorities on how solids travel over and through liquids, ranging from Daniel Bernoulli's *Hydrodynamica* (1738), which 'established the principles of hydrodynamic lift', to Lindsay Lord's *Naval Architecture of Planing Hulls* (1946), written for the US navy's motor torpedo boat programme by an ex-rum-runner, which proved that long is wrong if you want to plane fast.

Simmons also had a touch of the occult about him. According to John Elwell, who surfed with him in California, 'This guy had the power of "presence". You could feel it when he walked in… I… felt like a wind passing and he went behind me unseen. The guy wore a glitter of fiberglass dust and clothes of resin… He was poorly groomed and shaved and spoke in short, hard one-liners, snarling or cackling laughs. He was no nonsense, almost unfriendly at first. He was all business and a busy person about to die young.'

Elwell was with Simmons when he died surfing at Windansea, southern California, in 1954, at the age of thirty-five. He took off on a tall wave, slipped, was knocked out by his board and drowned. His revelations about surfboard shapes were all but forgotten for thirty years, when they were rediscovered by trial and error and his calculations confirmed by computers.

I drove to Westward Ho! in North Devon to pick up my Mini Simmons. My destination was christened after an abbreviation of the title of Charles Kingsley's novel

Westward Ho! Or The Voyages and Adventures of Sir Amyas Leigh, Knight of Burrough, in the County of Devon, in the Reign of Her Most Glorious Majesty, Queen Elizabeth, whose mixture of cod history, derring-do and tragic ending captivated Victorian England. Developers capitalized on the interest it had awakened in the region, hitherto known for its poverty and backwardness, and issued a prospectus for a hotel they wanted to build on a few scrubby acres of land in Northam Burrows. The prospectus exalted 'the salubrity and beauty' of the area, noted that Sir James Clark had 'placed it in the highest position for health-giving qualities', and name-checked the bandwagon it was trying to board: 'Professor Kingsley's "Westward Ho!" has excited increased public attention [in]... this romantic and beautiful coast.'*

Kingsley, who'd celebrated 'the everlasting thunder of the long Atlantic swell' in *Westward Ho!* – the book – feared the development would ruin the area and wrote a sarcastic letter to its promoters asking how their 'scheme for spoiling that beautiful place with Hotels and Villas' was going, and warning that 'you will frighten away all the sea-pies [oystercatchers] and defile the Pebble Ridge with chicken bones and sandwich scraps'.

---

* Sir James Clark was physician to Queen Victoria and reckoned to have killed the poet John Keats earlier in his career when treating him for a malady he'd diagnosed as caused by thinking too much. Clark put Keats on a diet of one anchovy and one piece of toast every day, and the poet died hungry and in agony from tuberculosis shortly afterwards.

The money was raised, the Westward Ho! hotel was built and villas and bathing huts sprang up around it. A links golf course was added nearby and the new settlement assumed the name of the hotel in 1867. I liked it at once. The sun shone, a sea breeze swept its streets and pine trees swayed and flowers nodded in the gardens of its spacious villas. Even the commercial area of its waterfront seemed cheerful rather than merely tawdry. You could hire proper surfboards and wetsuits as well as deckchairs and windbreaks, the chips in its kiosks looked good and there was only one amusement arcade. I've always been mystified by these institutions of the British seaside, built to steal pennies from children. They offer so little in the way of entertainment – and such long odds against winning even a pittance – that their only purpose can be to teach their customers how to be good losers.

I picked up the Mini Simmons from a surf school behind the beach. I had an instant's trepidation before I saw it, just as a bridegroom at an arranged wedding might feel as he lifted the veil of his spouse. In the event, I uncovered a hefty beauty. The woman at the till watched me closely and when I smiled she smiled too. Liz was in her fifties but appeared far younger. She had salt in her hair, an 'instructor' rashie over her wetsuit with her name on the front and the attitude of a Girl Scout leader.

'Are you going to ride it now?' she asked as I paid, and gave me a free block of wax when I nodded 'yes'.

'You've got about an hour,' she said, 'until the tide reaches the ridge.' I guess she read mystification on my face and added, 'Some people don't pay enough attention to it and break their boards'.

The tide was low and the sea a long way away when I carried my Mini Simmons to the beach. I had to cross a rampart of stones that ran as straight as a concrete causeway parallel to the sands. Although this looked artificial, it was natural, and was a source of local pride. Arizona has the Grand Canyon; Westward Ho! has Pebble Ridge. The Ridge is something of a shape-shifter, sowing stones in the fields behind it some years, snaking up the coast in others. The ancient custom of 'potwalloping', which involved cider drinking and clearing the fields of their scab of stones, was maintained by the village golf club until 2008, when it was banned by Natural England and Pebble Ridge designated a Site of Special Scientific Interest. Freedom from human interference has led to order rather than chaos. Although Pebble Ridge may now drift where it wishes and strew rocks at will, rather than embracing such liberation, it has stuck to the straight and narrow.

My new Mini Simmons was heavy and so wide I could only just fit it under my arm. The stiff cross-shore breeze blew it against me as I went barefoot over the stones, forcing me sideways. The wind had stripped the beach of sunbathers and whirred sand crystals into the face of anyone who looked its way. A few families huddled behind rented windbreaks in their swimming costumes. A sun hat shot past my feet, chased by shouts, but no one was willing to brave their skins against the gusts and grit to try to catch it.

I unloaded my board by the water's edge and a local surfer in his forties came over to take a look at it as I warmed up. He was slim, bearded, with rat-tail braids in his hair, numerous piercings, a stern face and a friendly smile. He nodded his head in time to music only he could hear.

'Mini Simmons?' he asked. He already knew the answer for he then told me that he was friends with its shaper, Dale Walker, who'd lived just down the road until a year or so ago when he'd moved to Hawaii, then Washington State, to test his new designs against the Pacific Ocean.

We spoke a little about whether I could duck dive it, and he suggested that if I started by twisting the nose to one side before pushing it into the water I could get it to sink before I was sucked up the face of the oncoming wave. He paused and we both looked out to sea where the waist-high swells were flopping rather than sucking.

'You could always just stand up and chuck it over the back of them,' he said.

I *could* duck dive it, and when I got to the break cranked it round and paddled to catch the first wave to arrive. I snapped to my feet and felt like I was standing on a kitchen table – rigid and rooted – then shot off the back of the board. It was fast as well as stable and thundered on ahead until my leash snapped tight and it dragged me by the ankle into the white water. Every new wave revealed fresh idiosyncrasies. If I slid a toe an inch too far forward at take off, it would pearl; to turn, I had to hunker down into a squat and grab the outside rail; and to go, slot the inside rail into the face of the wave like a letter opener and slip along sideways. The water sparkled as it peeled off the board and it became a game to hold it in position with my toes, pressing down to engage, or easing back onto my heels to keep it from cutting too deeply into the wave. At times, it felt like a speedboat rather than a surfboard: instead of curling round sections of the wave that had closed out, I motored straight over them; when the wave threatened to die, I'd stamp on my front foot and get going again.

When I paddled in, the breeze had died and white water washed the base of Pebble Ridge where it melted into the stones. I was suffused with wellbeing. The other surfers in the water had been mellow and since the break was composed of a multitude of small peaks, everyone had been sufficiently spaced out to catch all the waves they wanted. I was riding barefoot again, for the first time in five months, which felt uninhibited – as if my whole body rather than just my feet were naked – and the Mini Simmons had worked: had given me longer, faster, rides than I would otherwise have enjoyed.

I celebrated with some surf porn when I got home and watched *Morning of the Earth* (1971), a cult classic without a plot featuring bearded and barefoot surfers with dazed eyes, who drift round the frame like saints from the dark ages; a soundtrack rather than a script, complete with jazz flute solos; endless backlit, peeling waves with sparkling crests; emerald Balinese tubes; and a token shot of a seagull in flight, silhouetted against a blood-red sun. Its aims, according to its director Albert Falzon, were threefold: to recreate the beginning of the world, hence the aerial shots inside the crater of a Hawaiian volcano at its own beginning; to evoke the elation a surfer feels when dropping into an eight-foot wave and skating over a reef; and to teach people what life was really all about by showing them 'what this planet is giving to them all the time' – and which they were missing by watching films. I identified most with the shots of sparkling water peeling off rails, for the knee-tremblers I'd ridden that afternoon at Westward Ho! sparkled in my memory in the same way.

12
Down the Line

July 2016

We went to the house in Galicia for our summer holiday. The Texans who'd viewed it in March had decided to buy in the Ukraine instead of green Spain, and it had been shuttered up ever since. Wild boar were mauling the lower boughs of the apple trees in the orchard on the night we arrived. We could hear rather than see them and they sounded like cartoon hogs, grunting loudly and savagely, shaking the trees and crunching unripe fruit in their jaws. When I opened the side door to the house bats flew out, then followed us in and wheeled around our heads. As I hunted for the power switch to turn the electricity on, they passed so close to my face that I could feel the wind from their wings. The temptation to drop my torch and swat them away from me was strong. Bats are not as passive as their admirers claim. Although their sonar allows them to judge their position to the nearest tenth of a millimetre, they can still choose to bite. In some parts of Europe, they carry European Bat Lyssavirus (EBLV), a strain of rabies, and even a scratch from one can kill. A Scottish batworker died from EBLV in 2002, disproving – tragically – the myth that Great Britain is free of the disease.

The next morning, I took Rosy to the stream at the end of the garden and we met Paco, who lives a few doors down from us and whiles away his retirement by walking around the village. He slipped into Galego as soon as we'd finished the courtesies of greeting and started digressing immediately afterwards, so that he was hard to understand, and the question Rosy had asked me to ask him – if the village had, or had ever had, any wolves? – was answered only after the matter of whether the stream, el Colchon Fria, had had more trout in the past, which, apparently, it did, for he had once caught a hundred in a single afternoon, although it had been deeper then. And as for wolves, they say one had killed a goat, but where were the goats?

'Taken by wolves?' I suggested.

Paco shook his head. There had never been any goats. *Falta uno*. Carmencita brought a kid into San Salvador on the other side of the valley before she was married and a bear ate it.

'How did they know it was a bear?'

'A truck ran it over the very same night. It was the last bear in Galicia.' Paco raised his walking stick in salutation and resumed his circuit of Couzadoiro.

The stream would have made a fine location for a film about fairies. Damselflies and dragonflies flitted between the ferns that lined its banks. Finger-length spotted trout drifted in its iridescent waters and quartz crystals glittered on its slate bed. I admired the scene and pictured it locked in Rosy's memory – a golden instant from childhood, with halos around everything, which she might recall in the future when she was sad, that would make her smile again. Such memories are rare and are formed over a few perfect moments during a tiny portion of our lives, perhaps twenty weeks in total – a fortnight's summer holiday each year between the ages of five and fifteen. They are also hard for a parent to orchestrate, for the child might remember that the water was cold rather than being entranced by its clarity, and so develop an aversion rather than affection for the place, and shiver instead of wishing they were back there again if it surfaced in a dream.

Then we were joined by Onyx, the neighbour's Labrador, who'd jumped their fence in search of fun and needed no invitation to get wet. He issued a few joyous barks then leapt, paws splayed, tail aloft. The splash as he landed in the stream scared off the fish, sank the water boatmen and scattered the damselflies. Rosy fell in love at once and asked if we could take Onyx home, to England, she meant, and could he sit next to us on the plane?

There were waterfalls and rock pools lower down the stream, where it ran into a river at the bottom of the valley. Its falls had dug deep into the river's bed and hollowed out its banks. I put on swimming goggles and dived down. The cascade licked a curtain of bubbles eight feet deep, and trout fled through it into a cave at the bottom of the pool that was as deep again, with bronze walls and a bed of matted eucalyptus leaves. Downstream of the waterfalls, the river spread out for a stretch into a waist-deep swimming pool that was infested with leeches. We'd discovered them a few years before when we took the children there for a picnic and a dip. All was fine until little Hugo climbed out to get a towel from Anna who pointed at his legs and screamed. They were tasselled with slim brown ribbons that wriggled with life. Although it doesn't hurt when leeches latch on, they can be a frightening introduction to parasitical species, and Hugo started screaming too. We'd all given up smoking so instead of getting rid of them, Empire-fashion, by touching them with a lighted cigarette, we had to pull them off one by one. All the kids' legs were streaked with blood when we got home.

A mile further downstream, the river reaches the sea at Playa de Morouzos. I find this beach eerie, but I can't pin down why. It may be the black slate dust in its sands; the debris that accumulates there after storms – I've found a smashed-up navigation buoy, twenty feet in diameter, fragments of shattered fishing boats and large trees, complete with their roots, bedded in the dunes; the relative chill of its waters; or the speed of the shoreline currents that run even when the sea is calm. Foxes and wild boar scavenge its tideline after dark and leave a web of footprints over the sand. Birdwatchers lurk in the marshes by the river mouth.

You can wade out to an uninhabited island off the middle of the beach at low tide if the sea is flat. The island is shaped like a cake tin, with vertical sides and a rounded top, maybe a hundred feet tall by two hundred yards long. When the swell from the north is overhead or more in height, tubes appear on the sandbanks on either side of the island. Most close out but some peel. No one surfs Morouzos but it's the first glimpse of the sea you get when driving from the house to the coast and a great indicator of what might be happening elsewhere. If it's flat, drive south to Pantin; if there are little white horses – make for Esteiro; and if it's ten feet tall and slamming onto the sandbanks, go to the municipal swimming pool in Ortigueira.

We went to Esteiro for our first day on the beach. The bar in the car park had groups of old-fashioned Galego beachgoers beneath its umbrellas, dressed for cold weather. They drank small bottles of Estrella Galicia beer and sat with their backs to the dunes and the beach beyond. Seabathing was frowned upon in Galician tradition. They were great sailors, who disdained swimming – don't go out to sea if you can't trust your boat. Conservative attitudes towards dress, meanwhile – a favourite local proverb runs something like 'unless you want to die young in great pain, always wear your winter clothes in summer' – kept them from posing on the beach in Lycra swimwear. It was, moreover, lunchtime. Some ate a stew of tripe and chickpeas at the bar, others grilled beef on the bone at the barbeque pits under the pines.

There were honey bees and pale-blue *convolvulus* flowers on the dunes. The sand was burning hot and scorched the soles of my feet as I walked over to check the waves. The beach and break beyond it were inviting, and empty. Short blue walls kicked up, crested, then collapsed and span themselves into a froth of white lace. I couldn't wait to get in.

The sea was cool and limpid and as refreshing as a gin and tonic. Once I'd paddled into deeper water, I slid off my board, swam under, and stared at the sky through the surface. My vision was so blurred that everything solid in between – my board above, my hands pulling water past my face and over my shoulder to hold me down – were edgeless, undulating shapes against a blue and silver mirror.

The waves at the break were too steep for the Mini Simmons, but I found a spot to one side where refraction jacked up their faces, creating a runway that enabled me to get upright before they rolled over themselves, and I caught a few. It was curious to be surfing left-hand waves again, which are harder to ride if you're a regular footer, i.e. stand with your left foot forwards on your surfboard.* This is because they are falling behind you rather than in front of your eyes, and you have to twist your head backwards to see what's coming. The beach breaks I'd been riding in

---

* The alternative is to be a 'goofy footer' and stand with your right foot forward. Probably three quarters of surfers are regular footed.

England had usually offered a choice of left or right, and I'd favoured facing the wave that I was riding so much that my middle-aged flesh had adapted to the preference. When I looked over my left shoulder at Esteiro to gauge when to go for my first wave of the day, my neck clicked and then cramped up and when I managed to get onto my feet, I squatted like an ape in the middle of the board.

But subsequent rides and falls softened my muscles, and little by little I got longer and longer rides, zipping along down the line, watching the beach glide by. Each trip presented me with a short magic-lantern show – a series of slides showing people at play. Lunch had ended and a few of the more liberal Galegos had set up umbrellas and folding chairs on the sands. Tourists in shorts and bikinis emerged from the pine forest and began exercising, posing, playing games and playing dead on their towels. A few more boards appeared at the break, including a couple of local kids who'd clearly been held back until after lunch, for they flew at the waves with demonic vigour. Even their wipeouts were furious and I admired them and their energy: how wonderful to want to rip like a pro; how nice to have to endure nothing more than a good meal to go surfing.

It was bliss to surf more or less every day in beautiful places; to enjoy the warm weariness it generated in my body and the giant appetite it provoked. We'd choose a beach in the mornings: Playa Furada, reached by a zigzag cliff path whose slopes were covered with heather and bracken; Playa San Anton in Espasante, right by the village, graced occasionally by the presence of its mascot – Anton the pig, who the villagers spoiled as he was the main prize in the Christmas lottery and was replaced every year; Picón at the bottom of a cliff, with a bar at its summit that resembled a cross between a bunker and a railway carriage; and Bares, with its little hooked harbour and crystalline water.

Each sortie was an adventure in miniature on the tan and emerald fringes of the Atlantic. Rosy and I combed the rock pools, which were tenanted with miniature shrimps that would march onto our bare feet and wave their translucent, needle-like claws around in a kind of ecstasy. We found an octopus at Picón, clumps of hermit crabs at Barres, and had a seaweed bath in Espasante, where we wallowed in the mass of drifting fucus that had been corralled into a corner of the beach.

The mood out in the surf was relaxed everywhere we went. People chatted and gave waves to each other, with magnanimous gestures, as if to say, 'Take it! It is yours to love and spoil!'

There was a degree of black Galician humour in many of these gifts. Surfers would invite each other to ride close-outs and ankle bashers with as much, if not more, enthusiasm as good waves, and laugh at each other's wipeouts. It was a vast change from the crowded breaks I'd been riding in England, where on some days the surfers had behaved as if they were a pack of starving curs, baring their teeth and fighting over scraps. Here, in contrast, good humour prevailed. The hours passed in minutes. And, wave by wave, I rebuilt my skills. Both my balance and co-ordination started firing: I felt the energy of the wave through my bare feet on my board – and harnessed this rather than fighting it. Each wave was going on its own sweet way with me aboard. The trick was learning to stay with it and carve a path along its face with my rails.

We met Ness's cousin Miles and his two teenaged sons, Nicolas and Lucas, at Pantin. Pantin is the best-known surf beach in Galicia, home to an annual contest that sometimes forms part of the world professional tour. It's a beach break with a reliable peak that works up to about double-overhead in height. The sea there has a beautiful and distinctive colour that I've only ever seen elsewhere in the irises of a girl I knew thirty years ago: they looked emerald in some lights and sapphire in others, and always had flecks of each hue like the flaws in opals shimmering under the dominant shade.

Shore-side, it was all change at Pantin. There was a new double-storey café, built from stone in traditional style on the spot where the surf schools used to park rusting containers to store their wetsuits over the summer. Miles and his boys were waiting for us on the café's terrace. I hadn't met them for a few years and was astounded, and amused. The process of growing up is blindingly fast when seen through adult eyes. Turn your back on adolescents for any length of time and when you look again they're ten inches taller and bearded. Encounters with kids who've morphed into giants always make me laugh in wonder. I could still see vestiges in Nicolas and Lucas of the children I knew, and wondered if it were not all a joke: that the colossuses before me had pretended to be kids when we last met. I think they saw the funny side too, or had learned to hide their embarrassment when every adult they haven't seen for more than a year opens their mouth and trots out platitudes at them from a very short list – some condescending, others ridiculous, and all intended to remind them of a part of life they'd just left behind and, whether intentionally or accidentally, to put them in their place.

Nicolas is on the local surf team and rides with power and aplomb. Lucas is at the kamikaze stage and attacks each wave as if it was his last: in danger, there is glory...

We paddled out together then split up to search for the different things we wanted from Pantin. Miles had a long-board, Oxford-blue in colour, made by the local shaper whose brand is a *lion couchant*. He was an astute judge of surf. He caught the best wave of most sets and rode them all the way into shore, while Nicolas ripped the tops off the steep ones and Lucas aimed his board at the sky beyond their faces, fell, and came up laughing.

I didn't catch many waves. It didn't matter. A week of surfing in Galicia had given me more than clear water and uncrowded breaks. There had been times in England when I had felt that hope was wearing thin. The penances were numerous, the pleasures rare. Another day of traffic jams and crowded slop might have driven me to give up surfing altogether, sell my boards and target a different childhood ambition, like spearfishing for bluefin tuna. You have to shoot them in absolutely the right place, or you'll lose your arm with your spear, if you're not dragged down at fifty knots and drowned. Spearfishers train for bluefin by shooting tiger sharks, though I intended to skip this part of the dream. However, after a few days on gentle, reliable swell I decided to leave the tuna for later. The brief, clean rides that I'd enjoyed had such a sweetness to them, that they'd satisfied some deep desire that could not be measured in objective terms. I could have got the same sensation of speed by cycling, or sticking my head out of a car window, at thirty miles per hour; the same drop by jumping off a low wall; and spent far more time standing on a board in the sea if I'd chosen stand-up paddle boarding; but surfing beat them all. It had a combination of thrills that fired up my pleasure centres in a way that other leisure activities, and indeed narcotics, could not.

There's a *mesón*, a traditional Galician inn, on a bridge a few miles out from Pantin on the road to Cerdeira. It's an inviting place, built of rough stone blocks with white pointing. Lumps of quartz are cemented to the edges of its slate roof to hold them down during winter storms. The *mesón* has tables and varnished Oloroso barrels outside and its menu is composed of Galician delicacies and staples – *percebes*, *caldo*, *almejas*, *raxo*, *tetilla* cheeses, *pulpo*, *chuletón de buey*** – and vast loaves of brown bread shaped like flying saucers. There are casks of local Albarino and a wine list of Spanish reds that would please a connoisseur, including rare and strange vintages from Ribeiro de Duero and Priorat.

We had a farewell beer there after surfing and Miles told me that unless Pantin bans smoking next year it will lose its EU certification as a Blue Flag beach. Secondhand cigarette smoke is now judged to be as deleterious to water quality as untreated sewage. All beaches will be monitored for smoking and those that permit it will be downgraded. The local councils were cutting back on lifeguards at the same time as appointing smoking inspectors. New European directives required that a lifeguard needed hundreds of hours of experience and a qualification costing several thousand euros before they could be let loose on a beach. A properly trained guard – if you could find one – cost ten times as much as the college kids with keen eyes and adequate coaching who'd hitherto manned the lookouts along the sands. Although these young zealots had been a pain in the arse when they concentrated on their work, hoisting red flags if people tried to swim when the swell was only knee-high and calling the municipal dog catcher if you took your pet onto the beach, many were surfers who understood the sea and kept the beaches safe and clean out of habit, who were now

---

* Goose-necked barnacles, tripe and chickpeas, clams, spiced pork, breast-shaped cheeses, octopus and giant T-bone steaks.

destined to join the other forty per cent of their age group in Spain who were unemployed.

Miles has an innocent face and a cynical mind. He shares my fondness for dark Galego proverbs and suggested that the Junta had had '*El mejor nadador es el agua*' ('water is the best swimmer') at the back of its mind when it let go of its lifeguards.

Both Nicolas and Lucas wore surf watches, which told them the tides and monitored their movements while on the water. It had been a slow day: Nicolas had covered three and a half kilometres, Lucas just under three. When the swell was pumping, they regularly travelled five or six. It was fascinating to see surf sessions expressed as numbers as Lucas flicked through past outings on his watch. On average, he spent eight per cent of his time on the water surfing, forty per cent of it paddling and the rest waiting for waves. This, apparently, was an impressive ratio, similar to that of a professional in a contest.

'Does it monitor wipeouts?' I asked.

He shook his head. You could guess when they'd happened, he told me, from the heart-rate-monitor function, and called this up on the screen of his watch. This too was revealing. The biggest spikes in his pulse had occurred just after he'd finished riding a wave. Apparently, this is normal and results from a combination of exertion and lashings of adrenaline fizzing through the veins, that only catch up with the surfer after he's kicked out. Wipeouts, in contrast, peaked lower, but lasted longer.

Rosy, meanwhile, had fallen in love with Lucas and paid him court by talking at him and bouncing up and down in front of his face while he gobbled up a *beicon* sandwich made from a foot-long arc of Galician bread. She fell asleep as soon as she was strapped into the car for the drive home, and when she woke again the sun was setting over the rock pinnacles that marked Cabo Ortegal. I told her that these were all that was left of the witches who'd once terrorized Galicia, together with their demonic fox familiars called *raposeiros* that could see through walls and kill people with their howls. In the same year that Christopher Columbus had set off for America, the Pope had sent witch hunters to Galicia to clear it of the baleful pagan influences that had been active there since the days of Noah. The witches were many and well hidden. But each needed to sacrifice a child every year to maintain her black magic. The hunters spread a rumour through the province that a Barbary slaver would arrive on the coast at the next full moon, with a cargo of child slaves taken from Dorset.

The witches gathered on the cliffs. Christian priests and knights crept in behind them to stop them escaping. And as the full moon rose out of the sea a ship sailed into view, with a crowd of blond children shivering on its deck. The witches broke cover and ran down to the shore. The ship hove to and the children formed into ranks on its deck and, at the sound of an altar bell, sang a 'Te Deum'. Once the trap had been sprung priests emerged from their hiding places in the taff rails and hosed down the witches with Holy Water from the bilges. The witches were turned to stone, and all that is left of them now is their pointed hats, and the tips of their fox's tails, which form the Aguillons, or Pinnacles of Cabo Ortegal.

13
Cutback

August 2016

The sea around southwest Britain was calm for a week after we returned from Galicia. I managed my impatience by teaching Rosy how to fish in the harbour at West Bay. The fish spurned our lines but we caught a bucketful of crabs with the drop net. These, and an ice cream after they had each been named and returned to the harbour one by one, gave her the positive associations I'd hoped to create by landing a few mackerel. Every evening, I ran through the swell charts and long-range weather forecasts, hoping that one of the depressions forming mid-Atlantic might stray our way. Each time, however, a likely formation appeared, it dissipated far out to sea, or tracked north to deliver rain to Scotland. Although such a weather pattern was normal for late August, I was beginning to resent the long hours of sunshine and still air. I envied animals that could hibernate – fall into a state of suspended animation – when the season wasn't to their liking.

I got my skateboard out and practised turns on our drive. The caravan park below was out of bounds to non-residents over August. Every pitch was taken and the spaces in between filled with pop-up gazebos and washing lines, so that the twenty yards of asphalt between our front door and front gate were the sole resource available to me to keep my sense of balance alive. This was scarcely enough space to try to imitate a cutback, which was the next skill I wanted to master on a surfboard. When you shoot ahead of a breaking wave after take-off, and have to return to it before your speed dies and it rolls away, you need to make a U-turn, or a U-turn-and-a-half, known respectively as a 'cutback' and a 'roundhouse cutback'. Cutbacks were things of wonder in the 1960s, before such modern moves as aerial 360s were invented. Surfers shouted out compliments, or raged with jealousy when they saw someone else perform a good one. While *Surfer Magazine* no longer commissions photographers to capture epic cutbacks for posterity, the move is still fundamental to staying with the wave instead of stopping and sinking and wondering over what might have been.

My chance to work on cutbacks on the water came suddenly when a small, deep low appeared without warning on the swell forecast charts. The charts display wave height by colour, with royal-blue for calm, crimson for very high, black for phenomenal and a rainbow of other shades for interim sizes. The low resembled a sacred heart on my computer screen, with swirling lines concentrated around a blood-red cardioid splodge. The jade-green ring on its periphery, representing three-metre waves, was scheduled to make contact with North Devon the next morning, coincidentally the last day of the school holidays.

There were a number of breaks I could choose from, many of them at the end of narrow lanes, which would probably be gridlocked with holiday traffic. Woolacombe, where Trev Toes, the weather prophet, was based looked to be the best option. I hadn't been there since February 2012, when Ness and I and baby Rosy had stayed in a hotel we nicknamed 'the Overlook' after the haunted version in *The Shining*, on account of its long empty corridors and deserted function rooms. The Overlook kept going over winter by offering pensioners bed and breakfast at the modest rate of £40 per week. Rosy lowered the average age of its occupants by a decade and was treated with reverence. Old ladies' faces lit up as they tottered by, and when I showed her the goldfish in a rather wonderful tank in the reception they gathered round us like vampires to stare at her reflection and drink its youth. The surf, meanwhile, had been big and messy and cold.

Woolacombe had been an easy drive in memory, the waves looked good on its webcam and I set off with high expectations. These survived until I was twenty miles away, when the traffic turned stop-go for the rest of my journey. Tedium became torture as I inched down the hill into town, with a view of solid head-high waves breaking both right and left along its beach.

Woolacombe had the worst crowds I'd seen at any resort that summer. It had been cursed by TripAdvisor with the title of 'Family Beach of the Year' for the second year running, and so was overrun with families looking for the best for their children. The first two car parks were full and the third was closing in on its limit. Its entry fee was seven pounds, cash only. En route to a cashpoint in the village I noted that the same nightclub pricing was in force at its other car parks, whose owners – on the evidence – had formed a cartel to fleece visitors at a universal and extortionate rate. Their excuse, apparently, is that they have to make a year's income in two months, as if there was no other work available, even for the enterprising, throughout the other ten.

I passed a banner for Eyeball TV on the balcony of a pretty little flat above a shop. Was this where Trev did his divination – gutted chickens and scrutinized their entrails for signs of swells to come? The door was locked, there was no bell and no one answered my knock. Maybe Trev was in a trance and on a spirit journey, flying far out into the Atlantic, soaring over storm cells, making the sign of the cross over shipwrecked sailors, then zooming back, counting the wave period as he returned to his body...

Perhaps he'd just gone surfing.

The crowds pouring onto Woolacombe's beach were composed of atomized family clusters, bouncing off each other in a kind of Brownian Motion. They looked straight through me. My board – seven feet of purple fibreglass

– also seemed invisible. I had to dance around them along the grit track from the car park to the beach, weaving and ducking, and leaping and swearing whenever I trod on a pointed stone. There was a bottleneck at the steps down to the sands: people travelling in both directions were laden with folding tables and chairs and rolled up windbreaks, and there were repeated pauses as they struggled past each other with their furniture.

At low tide, the beach is long and thin. At high tide, it is huge. The tide was ebbing and people spilled onto its sands as the sea retreated. They'd come to play as well as lounge. Some were rerunning the 2016 Rio Olympics and there were stick and rock hurling contests, and foot races, with commentaries – usually monologues – to accompany the action: 'He's racing away! The crowd are screaming! He wins!'

My route crossed a game of cricket involving three generations – granddad umpiring, dad and uncle bowling and fielding, and three sons and a daughter aiming for glory with the bat. One of the boys connected as I jogged along the sands and the ball rolled past me into a thicket of windbreaks. Granddad waved his right hand and wiggled his fingers, as if playing a cadenza on an invisible piano – four runs for Jack. My next obstacle was the ramparts of a giant sandcastle that a man with the muscles of a builder, wearing cargo shorts and a tank top, was shaping with a full-sized steel spade – proper job – for his adoring children. Just as I thought I was through the crowds, I met a final challenge:

a gang of seagulls, who had stolen the ice cream out of a little girl's hand. I charged them and they were surprisingly bold. They had grown fat on stolen junk food over the summer and had learned how to intimidate humans. They tried to stare me down with their yellow, red-rimmed eyes, spreading their wings and snapping their beaks, and only flew away when my board was at their throats.

Woolacombe has a series of peaks that shift from side to side with its sandbanks. The banks are capricious but oscillate within predictable limits. The tides keep them in shape and in more or less the same places all year round. In September, they might all shuffle a hundred yards south; in March, sidle north by half the distance; and after a winter storm vanish altogether for a week or two then re-emerge overnight. Powerful rips run between the banks and these are key to the break.

I picked a rip, paddled and duck dived, and a few minutes later had reached my chosen peak. I felt as if I'd arrived in another country. Although the beach was overrun and the sea up to twenty yards out from shore crowded with swimmers and belly-boarders, their heads bobbing, skins glistening and limbs thrashing as they threw themselves around, there were only three other surfers in the right place to catch green waves. I'd expected crowds and was awed that so few had ventured through the white water.

It was not as if my fellow illuminati were superhumans, or even professional surfers. They were all male, all young: one who might have just turned twenty, wearing a beard and riding a longboard; another, younger, with a shaven head and avocado flashes on his wetsuit, paddling a Lost Pocket Rocket shortboard; and the third a teenager on an old, battered mini-mal. While I sat astride my board, trying to read the break and work out where to take off, we were joined by another surfer, who shook his head as he came towards us, pointed at the rumpus in the shallows, and said,

'Watch out for Teletubbies.'

The insult seemed apposite. It was as if the children's television programme of the same name, with its curious squealing creatures, Tinky Winky, Dipsy, Laa Laa and Po, that capered mindlessly around the screen like lunatics in the gardens of a Victorian asylum, had addled the brains of an entire generation, so that their world resembled a giant cartoon that raged around their peripheral vision in bright colours and accelerated motion, while they pranced about on the beach and built sandcastles in the eye of the storm.

The waves were powerful at Woolacombe that afternoon: the strongest I'd felt since Galicia back in March. The kids at the break were all competent surfers and knew the beach well. In order to conserve energy and maximize time on their feet, they performed virtuous circuits, surfing a wave until it met the rip, riding back on the outbound current, then paddling sideways to regain the peak. I picked the wrong wave for my first ride, which delivered me into a no-man's land of turbulent foam between two rips.

For the next ten minutes I felt like I was trapped in a computer game, where no matter how fast I ran, I travelled backwards. Wall after wall of white water came shooting towards me and there was only time to wipe my eyes, take a breath, and duck dive again before the next arrived. Fatigue soon dissipated the pleasure I'd felt at being out at the peak, at being a member of a small elite who got their thrills from riding waves rather than being amongst the Teletubbies on the sea's fringes. My disappointment was so intense that I was touched by defeatism. If I was tired now, then why bother surfing at all? The swells that afternoon were relative babies. Wave power doubles for every extra two feet of height, so I would have to be comfortable with four times the energy if I wanted to catch tubes. This little bout of self-pity restored clarity to my thinking. When you're stuck, as I was, in the impact zone, the only thing to do is to return to the shore and go back out with the rips.

I managed a cutback of sorts on my next wave. Rather than writing the symbol for infinity on its face with my wake, I added a scribble at its base that was erased by foam an instant afterwards. It felt good though. There's a certain magic when you trust yourself to lean far enough over to fall, then see your board carve round under your nose, restore your centre of gravity to the stability zone, and set you up to travel in a fresh direction.

The sea breeze arrived and made the waves easier to catch. The falling tide, meanwhile, had sucked some of the power out of them, and I found my rhythm: pop up, drop down the face, bottom turn, shoot down the line, cutback, then down the line again. The faces of the waves rose up to greet me as I flew along them, and when I strayed too far away I leaned and rode back towards them.

When I got home that evening, my neighbour Jim pulled into his drive as I was unloading my car. He took his golf bag out of his boot and we chatted across the fence, he with his clubs over his shoulder, me with my board and wetsuit at my feet. He'd just finished a round at Beaminster and was playing again tomorrow at the Dorchester Country Club. When Jim smiles, the expression rules his face – lines up its wrinkles and lifts them at the corners – while his eyes light up with unaffected joy. He'd clearly had a great time on the fairways. He said he'd seen a clip of surfing on TV when he was watching coverage of the golf at the Rio Olympics.

I told him it would be an official sport in Tokyo 2020. The news pleased him. I think it made me seem more human. Surfing had a bad reputation when he took up golf in the 1950s. It was an outsider activity and hence was considered a waste of time for those who wanted to get ahead along the straight and narrow road that they'd chosen. But now that it had been received as a sport by the International Olympic Committee (IOC), and its competitors would be rewarded with medals, my fascination was excusable rather than an aberration. I spoiled the news by nodding enthusiastically as I delivered it and a gush of nose-water sprayed out of my nostrils and splattered the plants at my feet. I don't think Jim had seen the phenomenon before, but he caught his face as it fell, said goodnight, and glided to his house over his immaculate lawn which was as smooth and even as the greens at his golf club. I pulled my wetsuit free of the brambles that were creeping out from the flower bed on our side of the fence, two-stepped around little mounds of dog shit, leant my board against the remains of a dilapidated bench, whose cast-iron arms had rusted and wooden slats rotted, and fetched a beer to go with the sunset.

Is surfing a sport? As soon as the IOC endorsed it surfers queued up to criticize them. Even competitive surfers, both past and present, came out against its inclusion in the Tokyo Games. Corky Carroll, the first true professional rider, a pioneer of contests, said it was 'too cool for the Olympics'. His antipathy was shared by other pros, who raised further objections. Surfing was an art that might only be judged by other surfers, according to the spirit of the age and prevailing conditions. If the waves were execrable and no competitor had surfed well, why award medals? Soul surfers, meanwhile, a category of wave riders who consider their pastime to be a form of worship rather than exertion, found the notion that it might be included in so commercial a spectacle as the Olympics abhorrent. Competition – per se – would be degrading while in communion with the eternal, let alone competing in front of a global television audience. Moreover, that people should debase themselves by watching surfing instead of going surfing was proof in itself of the fallibility of mankind, and not to be encouraged.

The drug testing, and indeed the gender testing, would also be demeaning. Imagine surfing being dragged into the same sewer as professional athletics? Would the IOC prohibit surfers from taking their traditional recreational drugs, and disqualify a competitor who bonged up some weed before paddling out, as they would for athletes in other disciplines? Would female surfers have to undergo intrusive examinations for hidden testes before they were allowed to enter the water?

I'm with the soul surfers. Sports require winners and losers, hence surfing isn't a sport. With the exceptions of professional surfing and character-building contests for juniors, the act – or art – of surfing has no rules, no points to score or concede, no clock to watch, no set distances to cover and there are no prizes. Unlike most other physical leisure activities, such as running, football, table tennis, weight-lifting, golf and cycling, there's no single objective that can be captured in time, distance, calories burned – and acknowledged with a click of a stopwatch or a ping on a Fitbit and celebrated with a mini fist pump. And outside the rarefied world of tow-in surfing on waves ten storeys tall, there's no teamwork.

The challenge, rather, is internal: do I really have what it takes to ride waves? To overcome the fear of getting held under and pulped, and of failing more often than succeeding? Surfing is both unpredictable and dangerous. If there is a contest, it's between the good and bad angels in your head. The 'bad' are masters of timing: they whisper, 'What the fuck are you doing here?' as you surface panting and heaving after a spell in the spin cycle, just in time to see another green wall approach to suck you up its face and throw you down under tens of tons of ocean. The 'good' angels, meanwhile, argue fortitude – 'If you don't try to fly, you'll fall' – which they back up with shame: 'If you're really feeling *that* feeble, then why not go home and buy a longboard and use it only when the swell is small and clean? Why not just *pretend* to be a surfer and get a campervan and some Quicksilver T-shirts?'

The notion that surfing is a private challenge is another point I have in common with soul surfers, although they take it to its extreme and believe that in a perfect world everyone would ride naked, alone, unwatched, by moonlight as well as in sunshine, where and when they felt the urge. For them, this is a matter of good manners as much as sound doctrine. It would be wrong to contaminate other people's quests by making a spectacle of yourself. The watchers might be tempted to copy you, and sacrifice their own creativity to imitation. I'm not quite such a purist. I think that on days when I can't get out because I don't have a board to hand or the sea's too big, that there is merit in watching other people riding, such as I had done at the Wavegarden in Wales. However, I find the sight abstract rather than aspirational, instructional, or symbolic. I couldn't imagine myself performing the same manoeuvres with such poise as the people on the waves, couldn't deconstruct their moves into numbered steps that I could learn, and didn't believe that witnessing the perfect backside vertical re-entry would teach me how to save my soul.

I was so stoked by my afternoon at Woolacombe that I tried to join *Surfer Magazine*'s Older Surfers online forum that same night. I'd found it via Google and its archives were filled with such irresistible threads as: 'Veteran's Quiver – Show Us What You've got!'

Mark from Ocean Beach had twenty-one boards that he claimed to ride regularly. Nathan in Byron Bay only had six from three decades of surfing. Each one was an avatar from his past. As he got shorter and wider so did they, and when Nathan stood his boards up in a line he could see the same changes in them that time had made to his body since his tall and slender single-finned Hobie from 1979.

I registered and found the forum was inactive. No one had posted on it for five years – or five eternities in web time. Maybe all its members had passed over into the twilight zone – were battling dementia, or cancer, and it had been allowed to lapse. Unless, of course, there was a more sinister explanation: the forum had been built as a deliberate dead end – a honey trap-cum-kill zone, where ageing and ex-surfers might pass their sunset hours online, reading the same things over and over again, while buying stairlifts and double glazing from adverts in the side panels on its pages.

There was surfing in my inbox: Miles emailed me from Galicia to tell me that his crotchety old shaper, who lived in a shack beside the storm drains south of La Coruña, had fixed a ding in the Mini Simmons (which I'd left in Spain) for ten euros, and that he'd insisted in being paid up front, as if it were a very great sum of money. The swell, meanwhile, had been good all week at Pantin. John, also in Galicia, sent a photo of a new painting he'd just finished, of a raven crouched on a seashore atop a mound of rotting cetacean flesh. He'd been longboarding on the Costa da Morte. I envied them both for living in an Eden, in the sense of a place without crowds – on either the roads or the beaches.

I took a break from web surfing to look at the stars outside and there were signs of change in the skies. The wind had switched and I could hear breaking waves echoing up from the beach, rather than the summer babble of music and voices from the caravan park. I was stirred by their sound. They were calling to me. Their message was visceral. I pictured myself as Nosferatu, gesturing with a pointed fingernail at a rising full moon and whispering, 'Listen to their music', as the wolves began to howl.

The music of breaking waves is complex and infinitely varied. It covers the full audible spectrum. Imagine a rock band, a choir of mermaids and an orchestra improvising together beneath an active volcano. The drums are the rumble of the shore-dump as it thumps onto the shingle*;

---

* The word 'shingle' is thought to derive from Norse or Anglo-Saxon and to be onomatopoeic: 'echoic of the sound of water running over pebbles'.

the bass notes the explosive booms as the air caught inside the breaking waves is first compressed, then blasts out through the spray; the vocals the sea gargling a throat full of stones – spewing them onto land then sucking them back; and the high sweet notes are the murmurs and trills of the white water as it rushes up the beach and sighs as it sinks into the sand.

The swell is forecast to build to overhead by the weekend. It will be preceded by heavy rains. The beaches will empty. The gulls that have overbred in anticipation of endless chips and ice creams will starve. Surfers and feral pensioners and their dog children will reclaim their kingdoms by the sea.

September 2016

Perhaps we're hardwired to love fickle things and part of the allure of surfing derives from its unpredictability. Last week's forecasts were wrong: instead of building, the swell faded. The data stream from the wave buoy in West Bay flat-lined; Des in Constantine sought to console via cryptic phrases in his forecasts, which hinted that his audience might explore life beyond surfing for a few days; and Magicseaweed couldn't offer more than single stars for anywhere on the south coast, and these at times and in places (say two a.m. on a Monday off Bovisand) that only the most ardent soul surfer might consider paddling out in.

There were, however, signs of hope for the future: the Met Office had offered its neck to the weather gods once again by prophesying a 'barbeque Indian summer', together with warnings that young children and the elderly should stay indoors lest they perish from sunstroke, a prediction that prompted the near-instantaneous formation of lows in the mid-Atlantic. 'Experts', meanwhile, warned the *Daily Telegraph*, that 'an invasion of 200 billion daddy longlegs' was approaching. Apparently, their larvae like their burrows to be wet then warm, and conditions this year have been perfect. Sergio, who ran a surf camp in the Algarve, once told me when I was travelling there that the Portuguese believed these insects were harbingers of big swell. They are adults for a maximum of only fifteen days of their year-long lives, during which period they cannot eat as they lose their digestive tracts when growing wings. When they cross into their final instar it is best if the ground is wet, so that they can lay their eggs more easily, and it seems that they can sense instinctively if storms are on the way.

When a couple of daddy longlegs blundered into the sitting room and crashed into the lamp the following night, I checked the wave buoy on Atlantic Station 62095, nearly a thousand miles to the west of Dorset, and found a nascent swell. The next day, the K2 Buoy, a couple of hundred miles closer, was jangling with fifteen-foot waves at twelve-second intervals.

I took Friday off work to go to Bantham. I glanced at the webcams before leaving home and they showed slow, regular, head-high waves. I took the Bonzer, which had been sitting in my office, waxed-up but unridden, for the last eight months. Pete Symms had insisted that the design only worked in bigger swell. Its bottom was built to create a state of choked flow and so take advantage of the Venturi effect and enjoy extra lift. But the flow only choked if it was flowing hard and fast. Anything less, and the Bonzer would behave like a bitzer – the Australian name for a mongrel dog that has bits of many other breeds in its blood. It was also reckoned to be a good board for cutbacks. Its long central fin generated massive lift in turns and its four 'side bites' – the smaller fins on either side – gave added control when you shifted from rail to rail.

When I arrived at Bantham two hours later the swell was still clean and sluggish but had halved in height. How would the Bonzer respond? Would it roll and stall like a log, nose-dive into the sandbars, or turn turtle and scarify me with its many fins? It proved easy enough to paddle, felt comfortable under my chest, and although I only had to duck dive once on the way out to the peak it was effortless in comparison to my Mini Simmons, which had required herculean strength to shove under waves and provoked a torrent of lactic acid in my deltoid muscles after very few dives.

I caught a waist-high wave straight away and the Bonzer, despite its reputation, flew: it planed quickly and slit the face of the wave like a knife once I got a rail into it. When I pumped, the huge concave seemed to pound the water together under the board and force short bursts of acceleration. I felt like I had springs in my heels. Best of all, it motored through cutbacks. I even performed them when I didn't need to and so discovered, by accident, how other surfers seemed to fly out the backs of waves when they kicked out.

In between zipping to and fro, I admired the beautiful orange colour of my Bonzer, and the profusion of seaweeds that drifted by. Was it autumn already underwater? Were all the fronds spinning past beneath my board the equivalent of falling leaves on land? As the tide turned the fucus became more numerous, until I felt I was afloat in a bowl of vegetable soup. Bladderwrack (*Fucus vesiculosus*) is said by both Japanese researchers and white witches to rejuvenate ageing faces, so when a handful drifted by I picked it up and took a bite. It tasted fishy – like canned sardines, pickled in brine. Its texture was a mixture of slime and gum and I spat it out after a couple of exploratory chews.*

Although the surf zone makes for disappointing grazing, it can offer decent fishing. Caspar, a university friend who moved to New York, told me that when they used to long-board off Long Island in summer the swells were sometimes so small that surfers took mini fishing rods out with them and cast spinners for bluefish. I asked if he'd ever caught one and he said yes, it was like a large mackerel with huge

---

* Fortuitously, as it happens, for it is also a powerful laxative, which would have been a nightmare in a wetsuit. Although the present fashion for seaweed in haute cuisine would have us put handfuls of it on everything, it is advised that bladderwrack is used 'sparingly'.

sharp teeth. It had bitten his hand – blood everywhere – then snarled his line around his leash. He'd had to paddle in, drag it out of the water, and kill it with a rock.

14
Offshore

The swell has been flat and the days are shrinking. I have fire in my eyes on my dawn and dusk commutes, for my route through Dorset is orientated east–west and, at this time of year, both the rising and setting suns lie across the crests on the road and white out my windscreen. There are crashes every week – abandoned cars in the hedges are as much a feature of my journeys as the dead wildlife along the verges. Wrecked vehicles, roadkill and crosses on many of the bends are invitations to meditate on mutability on my daily travels, especially as autumn advances. I find it a morose time of year. Although I love it for its swells and mists, empty car parks at the beaches, English apples and cobnuts, and frosts and bonfires and fireworks, I hate seeing the sun run away – hate it that daylight tapers week by week. And all the death in nature is dispiriting. I prefer soft green leaves on the trees to the shrivelling pre-shed shades of red that now rattle on their branches.

Autumn is a bad season for the middle-aged: the year is over the hill and so are we. The view down the reverse slope is disheartening and prompts black thoughts. Death already has us in its clutches but it will force us to witness our own degradation before it finally carries us away. It will make us look on with fading eyesight as our flesh becomes puckered and mottled and our muscles waste and skeletons creak, and may even spread the suffering over decades as we stagger downhill towards oblivion. We spend a large proportion of our lifespans expiring in comparison to other species. Instead of perishing in our adult prime like a daddy longlegs, beating our limbs to pieces against a light bulb, or tangling them in a spider's web in our desperation to find a mate, or starving to death in any event within a fortnight, we linger and fade. We haunt the space in time between youth and senescence, and the question 'Is that it?' or, strictly speaking, 'Was that it?' – expressing the disbelief that life could have turned out to be so bland – clatters around our skulls. At times, it seems that we remain alive only to give our children memories and to teach them, in turn, how to die.

My glum mood was compounded, indeed most likely inspired, by anxiety over an X-ray I'd just had on my right hip, which had begun to deliver searing bolts of pain whenever I was active, as if it, like my left hip before, had lost the cushion of cartilage between pelvis and femur and become bone against bone. It had been painful – on and off – for several months, but I had put that down, until the pain was more on than off, to all the exercise I'd been taking – surfing swimming, dancing – and I'd limped in to see the doctor. I'd been told not to expect the results of the X-ray for at least three weeks but it was hard to put it out of my mind.

To try to lift my spirits, I switched the car radio to Heart FM, whose upbeat playlist is composed, in the main, of pop songs for young lovers. The only moaning it allows on air is the passionate variety expressed in lyrical sighs, groans and pants in tunes like 'I Feel Love' by Donna Summer. Heart also offers prizes of up to £100,000 in its games, so that the contestants' voices shake with hope as they try to guess the name of a celebrity or attempt some similarly petty challenge. After half an hour or so of sugar from Heart, I switched to BBC Radio Devon, which also offers aural soma, albeit of a different strain. It is parochial and proud. Its presenters use Devonian slang so that there's always a chance of hearing a new word like 'gakeing' ('day-dreaming'). Its news broadcasts ignore international events and concentrate on cider-making contests or local road-improvement plans. In its more cosmopolitan moments it features stories from Cornwall.

When I got within ten miles of home, I switched to Wessex FM, a station so local that I know every one of its advertisers, from Long's fish-and-chip shop by the disused public lavatories behind East Street to Top Gear garage on the Beaminster road. Its playlist is a mix of 1980s pop and tub-thumping classics, say 'The Look of Love' by

ABC followed by Golden Earring's 'Radar Love'. Its traffic reports narrow their focus to a handful of roundabouts on the outskirts of Bridport and Dorchester, all of which are called by their nicknames – the George after the adjacent pub; and the Monkey's Jump at Poundbury, so named because it was once the site of Dorchester's gallows where criminals were strung up and twitched like monkeys while in their death throes.*

Upbeat radio stations and predictions of foul weather ahead in all of their forecasts lifted my black mood. It was time for a change of head. Instead of meditating on decline, I had to push on and be positive: autumn, after all, is a season of hope for surfers.

The waves should grow as we spin towards winter. There's a point towards the end of my commute home where the road rises and the sea appears beyond the land. That evening it was silver with an orange tongue beneath the setting sun. The water itself seemed solid rather than liquid, as if it had frozen over between the cliffs and coves that line the coast

---

* Public executions were popular events in and around Dorchester until the middle of the nineteenth century and the town had several sets of gallows. Thomas Hardy was taken to see Martha Brown die on one of them in 1856 when he was sixteen, and had her story in mind when he wrote his masterpiece *Tess of the D'Urbervilles*. Describing the event in a letter, written more than half a century later, he remembered 'what a fine figure' Martha had 'showed against the sky as she hung in the misty rain and how the tight black silk gown set off her shape as she wheeled half-round and back'.

as it curves around from Freshwater to Lyme and Tor Bay beyond. The sky high above had pink striations, its mackerel clouds indicating a distant low-pressure system to the west.

The chance to test my new resolve came soon. The low pressure that the corrugated clouds over Lyme Bay had foretold arrived, and two days later Magicseaweed was predicting a solid six feet of swell in North Devon. It was right: I spotted the waves in the bottom corner of my windscreen as I crested the hill behind Woolacombe and descended into town. The summer crowds had vanished. The cartel of car-park owners had dropped their prices. The seagulls were thinning out and those that remained looked malnourished and haunted by memories of feasts past. I parked in the front row of the best car park, just behind the beach. I leant on the chain-link fence that separated the asphalt from the dunes and watched the action on the water. On cue, a surfer dropped into a steep green wave that broke over his head and wrapped him in a tube for a fraction of a second as he shot off right-handed, then chased him along its face, lunging at his shoulder and sending white water snapping at his heels. I caught my breath. This would be the first time since my recovery that I was aiming to surf on waves that tubed, albeit in the loosest sense of the word.

The wind was blowing offshore, firm and constant. Off-shore conditions change the appearance of a break. When the wind blasts into the swells it physically holds them up, hollows out their faces and combs spray from their crests, which hangs in the air behind each one like a mane. It also tidies them into ranks, as if a set of lines had been ruled across the ocean. Most – if not all – of the shots of surfers used in adverts are taken when the wind is offshore. Who would buy life insurance on the strength of a video of someone flailing and falling in onshore knee-high slop?

The combination of offshore breeze and good swell is rare in southwest England. Both the prevailing winds and the waves that they create break headlong against its shores, and you can read their prevalence in the landscape: in the comb-over trees on ridges close to the sea; in the shingle banks on the south coast formed by longshore drift. The component stones of Chesil Beach in Dorset were licked out of the cliffs in Devon to the west, and continue to slide east towards Portland by a yard or so every decade. Hence offshore conditions make for red-letter days. At Woolacombe, there were knots of surfers at every peak all the way down the beach to Putsborough. I chose one and started paddling towards it. The journey out was easy. The rip was clearly defined, the sets were evenly spaced, so it was simply a matter of waiting for a lull then sprinting for a hundred yards, diving two or three times, and I was there. Once I'd reached the peak I sat astride my board to catch my breath. It was a different world – absorbing, exhilarating and edgy. The waves seemed tall as houses and the noise they made as they broke was tremendous – boom! – count to twelve – boom! – the chant of the deep ocean. The air was hazy with spray and wherever I looked there were rainbows of every size and state of completion, from arcs stretching for miles, to full circles the size of dinner plates haloing ruptures along the crests of the waves that were rolling in to die.

Wonders increased when I tried to take off. An offshore wind makes waves harder to catch: it funnels up their faces and shoves the nose of your board skywards at the same time that you're trying to push it down. Spray blasts straight into your eyes the instant the wave starts to pitch and, when you do pop up, the angle is steep and acceleration fierce, so that it feels like you're falling rather than gliding. You have to be far quicker onto your feet and in your moves.

I was too slow and was punished in double time. The wave, it seemed, had no patience for dawdlers and tripped me into its pit, dragged me up its face, then slung me at the seabed and collapsed on top of me. All this happened in the time it takes to count to two. I spent another ten seconds or so underwater, spinning backwards through the rollers of a mangle, with the sea rocketing up my nostrils. I remembered to wrap my arms around my head but forgot to open my eyes. Even though it's all a blur underwater, one should be on the lookout, as a matter of best practice, for the smudges of rocks or wrecks or other hazards, which can turn a hold-down into a stay-down if your limbs or leash get tangled in them. It's also a good way to be sure which way is up: in the chaos of bubbles and currents charging to and fro, you can't rely on what you see through your eyelids, for bright might not equal the surface.

I muffed a couple more take-offs, spent more time spinning in the green room, then gave up on the peak and tried to ride the smaller sets that broke on the inner sandbars. They all closed out and were nastier in their own foul way than their big brothers, shoving me into a ditch then jumping up and down on my head. After an hour or so of achieving nothing, I rode the white water in to the beach, bruised from my beatings and aching with disappointment.

Every time I went surfing, I believed that I'd enjoy a eureka moment during that session and be good at it forever thereafter. I was convinced that, one day, all my experiences would aggregate into competence, so that each time I paddled out, I'd be excited about the fun that lay in the session ahead, rather than apprehensive that it might reveal new shortcomings in my physical abilities, or my character.

As I wrapped my leash around my board, tired-frustrated rather than tired-exhausted, I noticed Lundy Island for the first time. It's a fair size – three miles long and nearly 500 feet tall – not far off the shore of North Devon, and I marvelled at how much space it took up on the horizon. It had been hiding behind a haze when I came to Woolacombe in the summer and this time I'd been so focused on my immediate surroundings at the break that I had failed to notice it. Apparently, it has puffins, a smattering of coral and no surf. I was also surprised to see deep puddles in the car park and streams of water running down Woolacombe's streets, until I remembered that it had been raining hard while I was surfing. Of course, the deluge from the skies had been insignificant in comparison with the maelstrom raging around me. But at one point, for just a few moments,

I had sat astride my board as the swells shunted under it
and admired the pattern that rainfall made on the sea. Its
droplets – anti-bubbles, with rainbow skins – bounced like
mini ping-pong balls on its surface before they coalesced,
each creating a perfect circle that radiated from its point
of impact.

What had gone wrong? Why hadn't I been able to catch
any proper waves at Woolacombe? Had it been a matter of
nerve rather than competence? Had my heart rather than
my reflexes let me down? My soul-searching prompted me
to investigate the nature of courage when I got home. I was
curious to learn – if it was known – where it came from
and where it went when it was needed most. By courage
I mean the decision to commit to a wave, rather than the
slow-burning valour of a Gandhi, or the white-faced fury
and superhuman strength of a mother protecting her baby.
Courage when surfing seems to me to be a sporadic, if
complex variant of the virtue, for there's seldom a binary
choice between go, be brave, and risk all; or go home and
blush in shame. There's no safety in fear, as hesitation can
have consequences every bit as painful as chancing your
neck. Indeed, on some waves you have to manoeuvre
yourself into such a position that the only safe way out
is on your feet. Why bother if you're scared and no one is
looking? Therein lies the conundrum: you can feel brave
right up to the critical instant, but sometimes a switch flicks

– a fuse blows – and you become weak at the moment that you need to be strong.

Courage has been observed and defined throughout history. According to Aristotle, it was a cardinal virtue, that everyone possessed on a sliding scale, bounded by vices at either end. If they had too little of it they were prone to cowardice; too much and they became reckless. In its perfect form, courage had a steadiness to it. Alexander the Great, Aristotle's most famous pupil, would not have pulled out of a wave on a whim. The notion that courage should be constant was adopted and emphasized by Christian philosophers, who turned it into a passive virtue. Saint Thomas Aquinas, quoting Plato, argued that it was defensive rather than aggressive, used to protect rather than attack: 'fortitude is more concerned to allay fear, than to moderate daring... Therefore, the principal act of fortitude is endurance, that is to stand immovable in the midst of dangers.'

This was of little help in teaching me to tame my hesitation at the instant of take-off, unless the point of surfing was to be chastised by waves, the bigger the better, until one submitted to the will of God. I next looked into medieval chivalry, but found it no more useful than Classical philosophy or Dark Age metaphysics in offering pointers towards self-improvement. In *Tirant lo Blanc*, a fifteenth-century masterpiece of Valencian literature by Joanot Martorell, whose subject is the way of the knight, courage consists of a mixture of superstitious guff and outright brutality. Martorell thought that children should be schooled in both from a tender age: exposed to mortal danger as often as possible, applauded if they survived, and the lesson sealed in blood.

I found parallels to my condition only when I came to modern thinkers. Søren Kierkegaard seemed, on a first reading, to describe the uncertainty I was feeling in his *Begrebet Angest* (1844).* Kierkegaard defined it as a kind of anxiety, such as Adam might have felt when he ate the fruit of the forbidden tree. Even though sin and guilt did not yet exist, God had warned Adam not to approach the tree of knowledge and he had disobeyed. If Adam had a mind at all, his first act of defiance must have revealed new possibilities to him, including that of uncertainty – how would his maker react? Hitherto his world had been black and white, henceforth it would be coloured with sin and death. However, whereas the existential angst postulated by the nineteenth-century Danish sage was an affliction that haunted its victims and shaped their behaviour over years if not decades, in my case it lasted only for milliseconds.

The explanation for my flightiness could be biological. The limbic shaft in the core of our brains – which we share with lizards – decides it's time for flight rather than fight, takes control of the body, and loosens the anal sphincter simultaneously to create a diversion – *caga y vete*,† as the Spanish say. There's nothing rational about it. The impulse

---

* Published a century later in English as *The Concept of Dread*.
† Translated literally as 'shit and split'.

is part of having been something else before we became human. The existence of this volatile throwback has been acknowledged in culture, often as a monster. Perhaps the dragons in tales of chivalry were metaphors for cowardice – the enemy within the kingdom that had to be slain on the quest for the Holy Grail.

I needed to rebuild my confidence and my next surf was at Lyme Regis, on brown, waist-high waves. Both Woolacombe and Bantham were onshore, overhead and messy, and looked like frothed-up cappuccino on the webcams, so I chose the beginner sets that I could see online at Lyme over the chance of one good wave and the certainty of frustration aplenty elsewhere. I parked near the Cobb, intending to paddle out through the harbour to the break, but it was the bottom of the tide and the boats were lying on their sides in the ooze within its walls. The water was colder and saltier than it had been in North Devon the week before, and almost completely opaque. I'd gone out without boots and seaweed streaming up from the rocks below tickled my feet as I waited for waves, reminding me that I had to fall flat when I came off.

There were a few other surfers in the water – some by the breakwater, others between me and the beach. Most of the time they were out of sight, hidden in the hollows of the waves, and the people on land seemed closer. Flanked to the west by the harbour, and with houses right down to the waterfront along Marine Parade, I felt as if I belonged to the seafront rather than the sea. The impression was reinforced by yellow buoys marked VISITOR moored around me. They rose and fell with the swell and when I put my head underwater I could hear their chains clanking on the rocks. Autumn leaves – oak, beech and horse chestnut – carried there by run-off from last night's rain drifted by, mixed up with seaweed.

It was a tricky place to catch waves. I was looking for little left-handers running down the reef outside Lucy's Ledge, but only one in ten broke cleanly. The angle had to be exactly right or the swell would lose sections on the banks further out, or get shoved sideways by backwash. But once I'd caught a few they became easy to pick and allowed me to correct some of the errors in technique that I'd been developing. I'd been grabbing my board by the rails at Woolacombe when I was trying to get up, instead of pressing down flat with my palms and pushing myself onto my feet. This habit is so wrong that it merits contrition, if not an outright public confession and a lengthy penance. When ridden by doubt, I'd tried to use the board as a shield rather than a sword – to force the wave away with it rather than use it to cut through the water.

At Lyme, my confidence ratcheted up every time I caught a ride, and as the waves became more manageable they also shrank in my perception, until I saw and rode them as they really were: pulses of energy, rolling through the sea. It became a game to surf them and so absorbing that any lingering angst vanished, together with the myriad of niggling, quotidian trivia that usually dart around my brain, emerging from the shadows now and then to derail a train of thought, and evaporating equally suddenly once they'd wrecked it. I was surfing for the joy of it, with no thoughts for anything beyond the here and now. It was a childish state of mind and all absorbing. I see the same in my daughter Rosy every day, for she thinks the principal aim of life is to have fun and, when she asks, 'Can I go out and play now?' I get flashbacks to when I asked my mother and father the same question, burning with impatience, ready to disbelieve whatever excuse they gave for saying no, and to fight noes with noes, or tears. It's a hard state of mind for an adult to recover on land, among all the distractions and petty tasks of twenty-first-century suburban living.

Two hours later the tide had changed and I was tired. Wind chill was biting my ears and fingers. I also felt lonely. Rain had driven people off the harbour walls and beach front, and the other surfers had gone in. I lay on my stomach and caught the next rush of white water into the beach. A couple waved at me from Marine Parade. I didn't recognize them but they were on my way back to the car, so I hobbled over. They were both in their late sixties, large and self-assured. He wore brick-red cords and a tweed shooting jacket; she a Barbour and a head scarf. Their faces fell as I approached. I think they were shocked by my age when I got closer – they had expected a portly youth rather than someone quite so grey and wrinkled above his wetsuit collar. She recovered her composure first and said, 'Henry took a picture of you on his smart phone. Show him, darling.'

Henry gave me a dirty look, but he was proud of his new toy and his mastery of its functions. He held it towards me at arm's length while he flourished his fingers over its screen and swiped through that afternoon's snaps. He had a few blurred seagulls, a couple of the fishing boats in the harbour, missing their masts where he'd zoomed in too close, one of his wife, just as a pretty girl in tight leggings happened to be walking by, and then me – shot of the day – riding a waist-high wave against a black backdrop of clouds.

It was the first picture I'd seen of myself surfing since the iPad videos that Rick had taken at the Wavegarden in Wales. In the spirit of being grateful for small mercies, I noted that my board was pointing in the right direction along the wave, and that I was standing up on it. My style, however, was abominable. If I'd adopted the same stance on the street fingers would have been pointed and voices raised in alarm. My head was slumped backwards, facing the sky. Henry zoomed in on my face and the resolution was high enough to show that my tongue was hanging out of my mouth. He zoomed back out and I gasped. My right arm was bent sideways at an unnatural angle. This trait is a recognized defect in style and I was ashamed to discover that I had it. It's called the 'wounded gull' after Mark Richards, four-time world champion in the 1970s, the most radical surfer of his age, who flailed one arm as if it was a damaged wing when he drove into his turns. The purists of the era could not forgive him this quirk, and even though Richards went higher, faster and deeper on the waves than his contemporaries, he is remembered as much for his unusual posture as for his achievements in the water.

Style when surfing – the ability to write a poem on every wave, to do something gracefully that most people can't do at all – is elusive and prized for being rare. Surfers commit many other crimes against elegance besides the wounded gull. The most common of these is 'stink butt', Californian slang for surfing with your bottom in the air. At least I wasn't guilty of that offence. Nor was I a 'bus driver', a surfer who rides with their arms outstretched in front of them as if holding an invisible steering wheel; or a 'teapot' who impersonates their nickname by making a spout with their leading arm and a handle with the trailing one. Besides, style was a small thing to worry about. As I thought about the sins I had committed, and those that I'd avoided, I realised that I didn't care how I looked when I caught and rode a wave.

People who love singing but who can't hold a tune still sing.

15
Lava Rock Reefs

November 2016

Storm Angus, the first named storm of the Met Office's 2016/ 2017 season, stripped the trees of their autumn colours overnight. The Axe valley flooded and run-off turned the sea an ugly shade of brown. Most surf breaks were blown out. A morning session at Lyme Regis felt like trench warfare, with mud-coloured swells chucking weed and flotsam around my head. I drove home wearing my dressing gown over my wetsuit, feeling old and tired – as if I'd just participated in some dull but worthy activity whose discomforts outweighed its pleasures.

I stumbled on the top half of a wild rabbit on the porch beside the front door when I got back. It had been so neatly divided that it was hard to believe that the cat had dissected it on his own. His teeth are sharp but small: needles rather than razors. Perhaps his surgery had taken him all morning. I found him asleep in my office, curled up under the radiator. To judge by the bulge in his midriff, most of the rest of the rabbit was inside him. Stan loves autumn. When the leaves drop and the undergrowth wilts his prey loses its cover and their young, living through their first fall, do not notice its absence before they're struck down. Meanwhile Stan's coat is growing thick for winter, and when I stroke his head his amber eyes glitter.

I checked my emails and found one from John in Galicia, saying they had five metres of swell from the north and that some of the local breaks which otherwise slept had come to life. He'd been out at Santa Caterina that morning, which offered long, green, glassy walls that peeled along a sandbank running parallel to the shore. You got out of the water and walked back up the beach to the same starting point after each wave. It was like riding a helter-skelter at a fairground: trudge up the stairs, then whoosh back down in a fraction of the time, and I imagined being there – hair flying, eyes watering – singing out in excitement.

The contrast between his morning surf and my own was stark. If the coming winter was going to be wet and windy like last year's, I might be shore-bound for weeks at a time. It was an ugly prospect, not least of all because I'd made so much progress with my surfing. I could paddle into a reasonably-sized wave with confidence, pop up, bottom turn, trim and cut back. My balance was still suspect and style abysmal, but I'd chosen to leave style for a future life. I was ready to step up to the next level of competence and worried, again, that my advances would be lost through enforced idleness. Surfing can resemble one of those needlessly brutal children's games that send you back to the start if you land on the wrong square just in front of the finishing line. I felt that if I sat around too long, I'd have to go back to riding white water, instead of moving towards the object of my quest.

There were other clouds on the horizon: although only November it was already Christmas on the streets, on the radio and on the banners and sidebars of web pages. Soon it would be impossible to avoid the slob-fest and hard to find any time to get out on the sea – in the event that rideable swells appeared. I'd also had the results back from the X-ray on my right hip. According to the radiologist, I had a lesion on my femur which was 'impinging'. When I asked my doctor what this meant, he explained it could be a number of things, ranging from a minor, if persistent irritation, that would subside over time, to a growth on the head of the bone, that was scouring out the hip joint and would need surgery to remove.

This bad news was compensated for by some good news in disguise. A customer cancelled an order, leaving me without work for the next week. I emailed friends to ask them where might be a good place to keep my surfing alive – and hopefully take it further – within easy reach of England. Tim said Morocco – Killer Point – and to watch out for orcas in the sets. Jason, Ness's cousin, invited us all to come and stay in Mexico: he had waves on his doorstep and Puerto Escondido, with its dredging, board-snapping beach break was only an hour down the Pacific coast. Miles advised me to go to the Canaries: the waves were both excellent and consistent; the people were amiable; the culture was laid-back, and if I wanted guiding or instructing there was always JMC (Juan Manuel Cabrero), a friend of a friend, a noted charger of big waves, who worked out of Caleta de Famara in Lanzarote. I found a flight there with Ryanair for £45 return, and got in contact with JMC who confirmed he could help me.

I'd been to the Canary Islands once before and had marked them as places to revisit. I'd even surfed there, albeit on a thirty-eight-foot sailing yacht, racing from Gran Canaria to St Lucia in the Caribbean, rather than on a board. It had been a thrilling experience. When we cleared the lee of the islands we hit an acceleration zone where the wind blew a steady twenty-five knots at 150°. We set the spinnaker, the stars came out along with a new moon shaped like a toenail clipping, and we surfed through the night, taking two-hour spells at the helm. I remember the adrenaline spikes as I bore off down waves, feeling the boat take off and watching the numbers surging on the speedo each time she started planing. Every so often I'd snap a glance at the wind indicator on the top of the mast and come back up little by little, not so fast as to broach, and not so slow that I'd Chinese gybe when the apparent wind spun back aft, feeling the boat through my feet and via my fingertips on the wheel – press, release, press, release – maintaining the dynamic tension.

*

Forty-eight hours after booking my flight I was sitting in the Hamburgueseria de Famara in Lanzarote, eating stewed goat, drinking volcanic Canarian red wine and reading Lermontov's *A Hero of Our Time*. The novel is a beautiful exercise in irony that shows how boredom can be as much of a spur to action as passion. Pleasure is fleeting: move on the instant that it palls and save regret, or guilt, for the grave. I wondered how its Byronic hero Pechorin, a wealthy and stylish misanthrope, would have kept ennui at bay had he lived in the twenty-first century. Would he have found his thrills as a mercenary, a hedge-fund manager, a Silicon Valley coder, dreaming of unicorns, or as a professional sportsman – riding Derby winners, dominating cage fighting – only to throw it all away? Might he have discovered redemption in surfing, and wandered the world on a yacht, searching for new breaks, testing himself against the ocean, far from the sight of detestable humanity?

I'd arrived in Lanzarote that morning and had spent the afternoon learning how to surf the reefs just in front of Caleta de Famara, the fishing village where I was staying on its northwest coast. The view from the sea had been stupendous. The eastern horizon was walled by Los Riscos, a near vertical band of cliffs several thousand feet tall, whose faces changed colour from green to red as the sun passed through the sky. To the north lay the island of La Graciosa, whose hills rose from the sea like inverted Us, such as a child might draw. The water underneath me was so clear it seemed that the lava rock reef below my board was only inches from my toes, but when I stuck my head under to check I saw we were in eight feet of water. The seabed was black and bronze, turning to indigo where it dropped off into the ocean.

JMC had arranged me a guide, Manuel, who lived to surf. The Hamburgueseria had a photo of him on the wall just inside its front door, making a bottom turn on a twenty-foot wave with a blue face and a white lip that reached out over him as he carved back towards it. If you looked closely at the picture, you could see his smile. This was his default expression. It was, however, no contrived grin, manufactured for the photographer who'd snapped him on the way into a tube. Face-to-face, he appeared amused, yet detached. Day to day, he spent more hours focusing on moving water and the insides of waves closing over him as fast as they could fall, than squinting at screens, like most of his peers. He lived in real time, looking at real things, and it showed.

We'd paddled out to the break through the mouth of the port, from which a deep channel led to the back of the reef. Manuel told me to aim at the shore when I took off, bottom turn straight away, and if I wiped out to swim parallel to it *rápidamente* when I came up and so escape into deep water. The break was left-handed and I felt awkward and lopsided when I turned into my first wave. I wobbled to my feet and stood tall, as if I'd been hardwired to repeat this elementary mistake. Perhaps too few of my ancestors were shot in the trenches.

Manuel paddled over as I scrambled back onto my board

after my wipeout, smiled encouragement and said that I'd looked like Christ when I spread my arms in a last, desperate attempt to stay upright. But, he added, we can't walk on water. We have to ride.

As the tide rose we moved along the point and came to a beautiful little peak called El Muelle, which offered mostly right-handers, the biggest of them just overhead in height. The rides were wonderful, even if they did not last long, but I caught plenty of them and the paddle back to the break was short. My confidence soared. Rather than riding one well, then losing my balance on the next, or realizing that I should be pumping just in time for it to slide past, I chased along their faces. It was fine, too, to play on the same small patch of sea the size of a football pitch with thousands of miles of emptiness to the west. All I had to do was triangulate three close points on land when I returned to the peak after a wave and I'd be in the right place every time.

The sets arrived at random. Sometimes I'd wait five minutes for their lines to appear, and these were hard to spot as they rose out of the deep water. At most of the beach breaks that I'd been surfing in England there were outer bars and bulges on the seabed, which pushed the waves up a hundred yards or so further out from where they broke, indicating that they were on the way. Here, however, there was no more than a shimmer, until the wave was nearly with you, whereupon it would rear up and, if it was too big, you'd have to dash towards it, duck dive under it and escape out the back.

I could see a point break further up the headland and, although less than a mile away, it was clearly twice the size of our spot. When I asked Manuel about it he told me it was called San Juan and that he'd been out there already at seven in the morning. It was great fun, he added, but you had to pick your waves carefully, as some sucked the reef dry before breaking on them, and trying to surf bare rocks on a fibreglass board was a *tontería* – a fool's errand.

Accommodation had been arranged for me in a shared flat in Calle Pasamano. It was on the edge of Famara and had vacant plots surfaced with crushed black pumice to either side. The other tenant introduced himself as Nazareno, and told me to call him Nacho. He had a surfer's build and shoulder-length curling hair, streaked blond by the sea. His voice had the musical accent, slow speech and dissolved consonants of a South American. I asked where he was from.

'Argentina.' he said. 'What about you? Where did you learn Spanish?'

'*Tarifa, y en la puta calle,*' I responded.* He winced at my slang and asked if there were good waves in Tarifa.

No, I told him – only beautiful, hollow, closeouts.

'Then why did you live there?'

'For the nightlife.'

---

* A coarse way of saying that I was self-taught, and best translated as 'in Tarifa, in the fucking street'.

Nacho brewed himself some *mate* and told me that Famara after dark was *tranquillo*. He'd injured a knee on the reef so was on surf-shop duty, dispensing wisdom, boards, wax and T-shirts, and playing reggae on the PA while he convalesced. His recuperation regime also featured gentle swims, medicinal hashish and early bed.

The air was so mild after England that I was restless and when Nacho retired I walked out and found a bar around the corner at the Famara Social Centre. It was a mellow place, built in the Franco era out of whitewashed concrete, with a view towards the sunset beyond the municipal skate park and the humps of distant calderas. Inside was a bar-cum-restaurant consisting of a pair of linked rooms, with an atrium beside the door that housed a banana plant, a prickly pear cactus and a miniature dragon tree.

The bar had black-and-white photographs from the 1950s on its walls, most of them of the fishermen who used to rule the local economy. One showed a group of these beside the port, carrying an icon of the Virgin on their shoulders, watched by their wives and children. All the adults in the photo were young, slim and barefoot, their faces alert, their expressions suggesting that they were concentrating on getting the ritual right. The faith, or acknowledged futility required to parade a wooden carving around the village – as their ancestors had done for centuries – must have instilled a sense of duty into them. There is also a hint of resistance in the eyes of the fishermen in the procession. Living under a dictatorship on the edge of nowhere, the ceremony allowed them to assert their identity, and show that although ruled with an iron hand, they were not yet slaves.

There were card games on the go inside the social centre: two hands of four, smiling red faces, raised voices and cards slammed down on the table as the players shouted out their names:

'The Eights of Swords!'

'The Tens of Gold!'

'The One of Cups!'

Spanish playing cards have three different suits from our own. Cups replace hearts, gold coins diamonds, and swords – *espadas* – spades. The suits have the same medieval symbolism. Cups are chalices and stand for the church, or when single the Holy Grail. Gold coins represent the mercantile class and swords the gentry. Clubs are just like ours and stand for the same estate – the peasants. When you watch a hand played with Spanish cards for the first time, it resembles a high-speed mutual tarot reading.

I wrote Rosy a postcard and drank more volcanic wine. This was the first time I'd ever written to my daughter, and I found it hard to know what to say in so small a space that might make her hear my voice when she read it. I told her about the waves and calderas and cliffs, and that I missed her, and I'd try to bring back some blood-red sap from a dragon tree. The wine meanwhile was working its way into my veins and nose, and living up to its Shakespearean reputation as a stupefacient for low-lifes. In the words of one of his prostitutes, Mistress Quickly, 'canaries' was a 'marvellous searching wine, and it perfumes the blood ere one can say: "What's this?"' It was the perfect end to a day at play in the sea.

I walked around the village the next morning before going surfing, and admired its dogs. They seem to be descended from a limited gene pool. The Caleta de Famara archetype is sandy-haired with a square head topped by a silver quiff, dainty jaws, a sausage body and delicate legs like a fawn's. They are small, quiet and discreet. One followed me down to the port, pretending to be my pet so it could take itself out for a stroll. Manuel had its clone in his car when he picked me up and drove over to Playa San Juan – the break I'd seen from El Muelle the day before. The dog tiptoed around us while we looked at the waves and crept behind a bush to cock its leg.

Manuel told me he'd been riding tubes yesterday evening over at a big wave spot named La Santa a few miles to the west. He'd filmed some on his new GoPro camera – a 3-inch cube of black metal and precision optics fixed to a snorkel mouthpiece. He shoved it between his teeth to show me how he used it and snaked his head from side to side, as if he was inside a wave.

I asked if he could breathe through it and he said 'a little' and looked puzzled by the question, as if that had been the last thing on his mind. Clearly, he'd had more pressing matters than respiration to attend to at the time. His tube shots needed editing so he played me some drone footage on his iPad of La Santa breaking when it was on form.

It looked exhilarating – and terrifying. The sequence started with the drone five hundred feet or so into the sky, looking down on a surfer lying flat on his board, alone on a sapphire sea, an icon in the centre of the screen. Then the shot panned in as the drone dived down and the sea humped up behind the surfer. When it lifted off the reef it changed colour to turquoise and boiled at its base. The surfer dropped in, went left, got tubed, kicked away, then drove back into the wave as it walled up for a second section, sucking water off its lava bed. When it started pitching he vanished into the foam and didn't reappear. Artistic shots followed of creamy white water flowing in over the reef, and foam from the prior wave running back out towards it. I was reminded of the head on a pint of Guinness, where white bubbles rise and the dark liquor drains down through them.

I shaded my eyes and stared at the break in front of me at San Juan, trying to gauge the height of the waves. Were there any freaks out there that might leave me riding rocks? I could just make out a couple of surfers as they took off and drew white lines under crests. The biggest sets were taller than a standing man holding an arm above his head, which can mean anything from three feet to seven feet, depending on where you are surfing. Hawaiians and Australians measure waves from their backs, which are half the height of their faces, so would have said it was three feet at San Juan. If you meet a surfer from either place, and they invite you to a spot where it's eight feet and pumping, imagine a line of a hundred double-decker buses bearing down on you side by side. Similarly, if a surfer from Brighton talks about six feet, think of a similar number of Robin Reliants kangarooing your way, crashing into each other at random, and breaking down on you the instant you get going.

Surfers who ride small waves can be rampant foot fetishists, always willing to add another twelve inches to the height of their local breaks. In contrast, those who surf bigger swells tend to follow the Greek philosopher Protagoras, who asserted 'man is the measure of all things'. They use a human scale – waist-high, chest-high, overhead and double-overhead – before they start talking in feet, and then only in increments of five or ten – fifteen feet, twenty feet and so on. In truth, there's no need for confusion: a global standard for measuring wave height exists, used everywhere by oceanographers, mariners, coastguards and all others who venture over the abyss, called Significant Wave Height, or SWH. Although it lacks the human element, it's clearly defined as being the mean wave height in feet or metres, of the highest third of the waves observed, measured from peak to trough. Its aim is to warn seafarers of how big waves might get rather than how small most of them will be. If your eyesight is keen, there's a rough and ready way to determine SWH from shore, formulated by Willard Bascom, the eminent US hydrologist: 'stand on the beach… at such a level that the top of the breaker is exactly in line between your eye and the horizon. Then the vertical distance between eye and backrush curl' at or below your feet 'is equal to the height of the breaker.'

*

The swell at San Juan was falling. When I applied the Bascom method, I reckoned the waves to be four to six feet tall, or chest-high to touching overhead. They grew again as I paddled out. Surfing gives you the field of vision of a child, and when you're lying prone on your board you enjoy the same limits to it as when you'd just learned to crawl and a sofa appeared to be as big as a wall. The break had two peaks about a hundred yards apart, each offering long lefts and short rights. It had a similarly grand view of the land as El Muelle, but from a different angle. The lip of the extinct volcano over which I was floating curled around the southern horizon, so that when I turned towards the shore and took off, it seemed that I was plunging into a crater towards the centre of the earth.

My first wave was head-high and I had the pleasure of watching it curl over me like a cobra as I crouched down after take-off. Then I took the wrong line, strayed in front, and was left riding foam over a shallow reef. Although the white water was as beautiful close up as it had appeared in the drone footage, with tints of glacier blue in its foam, it was a serious hazard. Even the small sets were powerful and there wasn't much space between froth and lava. If I messed up my duck diving on the way back out, I'd bleed.

My first dives were good and the waves were gorgeous as I slid under them. Each dragged a silver curtain of bubbles beneath it, which fizzed in my nose and ears as I passed through them. The water was clear and full of light. The surface overhead resembled a sheet of molten glass that stretched and pitched with each passing swell. Once, however, I didn't dive deep enough, and saw the reef shooting away below, as if I'd been grabbed by the heels and dragged backwards. I hung onto my board and got spun around its axis. When I surfaced, panting hard, heart pumping, hands shaking, I found the set had passed.

Manuel was waiting for me back at the break and said, '*Patito malo*' – 'Bad duckling'! I was lost and wondered if his endless smiles – he was beaming now – indicated, sometimes, insanity. Then I realized he was referring to my failed duck dive, and smiled with him. I liked the simplicity of the literal translation of 'duck dive' in Spanish and its diminutive form, which implied that a good *patito* was something that five-year-olds slow to develop co-ordination might master on the second attempt, rather than a physically demanding manoeuvre that had to be performed with split-second timing to prevent the risk of cracked ribs or a broken neck.

The sets at San Juan were widely spaced, and Manuel and I talked in between them about the fish zooming around the reef beneath us. I recognized bass, gilt-head bream and mullet from their shapes and flashes, but missed the *cantarero* (scorpion fish), which Manuel told me were teeming on it. They were the best fish to eat in the world, he said, but so flighty that they might only be taken on a long cane rod with a crab bait presented on a gossamer line. Hunting *cantareros* was a recognized obsession in Lanzarote, that afflicted middle-aged men who neglected their boats, their families and their dogs to wander the coastline in pursuit of the fish. They sent off to Tenerife for their equipment and pawned their furniture to pay for it. They pinned chicken carcasses over the reef at low tide to fatten the crabs they used for bait, which they tied to their hooks with silk thread before looping them into the water a metre or so uptide of where the *cantareros* were feeding.

The reef nibbled me once during a failed duck dive. I had dribbles of blood on my toes when I got out the water. I'd felt the cuts as they'd happened but little ones don't seem to bleed much when you're in the sea. My right leg, however, was not so good. The lesion on my femur that had shown up in my X-ray was impinging in earnest. I'd had searing pains in my groin and along my thigh all afternoon when I sat astride my board. These struck again when we got back to the beach and I peeled off my wetsuit. I had to sit down and drag it over my ankles as it hurt too much to stand up and step out of it. Manuel found something to look at on the break while I wriggled in the grit, resembling a flayed rabbit.

I ate that evening at the Famara Social Club as the sun set behind the skatepark and children milled around outside. A couple of its tables had been taken over by a surf-school class from England – four girls, three boys, all in their twenties, together in a bubble, fresh to the dream of riding the waves that they'd seen in adverts and placed in their lists of adventures to be had before they settled down. I envied them their enthusiasm and delight in minor triumphs on the white water. I questioned their commitment when one said it wasn't yet as good as their weekend waterskiing on Lake Windermere and others nodded in agreement. Would any of them become converts to surfing and rearrange their lives around the storms and tides? Or would they choose a skydiving course for their next adventure holiday? Were they the spiritual heirs of Pechorin, heroes and heroines of our time, cursed to be restless, never satisfied?

Two of them had ordered the fish of the day – *cantarero* – and I squinted over my book when the waiter brought them out, keen to see what these fabled creatures looked like. Were they so big that they were served in slices – or did you need several to make a meal? The *cantarero* looked strange enough to merit fascination when they arrived. They had been deep-fried whole and resembled small, shaggy grouper with oversized diamond-shaped heads from which their eyeballs had exploded, and a row of crisped and curling fins over their backs. Their bellies stood out, as if they hadn't been gutted before being cooked. They were received with surprise – and unease. The table fell silent and the pair of thrill-seekers who'd ordered them looked at each other. Might there be an excuse to send them back? Their discomfort was compounded as the waiter brought the next two orders: half a chicken, garnished with a mound of chips which spilled off the plate when he set it down, and a bowl of stew a foot across and eight inches deep that came with another bowl of new potatoes. The disparity in portion size was striking, and this gave one of the *cantarero* eaters an opening.

'What size is it?' he asked, pointing at the fish and then the other dishes.

'Normal,' replied the waiter – just out of his teens, neat, quick and fluent in four languages – and left to get the remaining orders.

Caleta de Famara has five miles of fine sandy beach, curling eastwards from its port towards the shadows of *Los Riscos*. Apparently, the sand vanishes every winter and returns in spring. Some migrates to the streets of the village, the rest is carried up the coast by the currents, then back again as the seasons roll by. It had yet to start its annual exodus when I surfed there and the thumping, overhead break on the beach had a blond tinge to its white water from suspended particles of sand. Swimming is banned when the surf is running and the red flag flying. I watched as a group of tourists in swimsuits ventured in and a wonderfully officious lifeguard roared up in a 4x4, blew a whistle, and ordered them from the water with a loudhailer: no ifs, no buts, no questions, no protests – get out, now.

While I was limbering up on the beach, trying to click my leg back into place, and pretend that the lancing pain in my hip had been something I'd dreamed of in my sleep, a surfer came out of the sea holding the back half of his board in one hand, which was still attached to his ankle by his leash. The break where the rest of it had been snapped off was strikingly clean – as if the board had been divided by a guillotine. He undid his leash, dumped the tail on the sand and went back to the water's edge. Presently, the front half washed in.

Manuel had pointed out a couple of peaks to aim at and a rip that ran between them, but even with such guidance it was hard to get out. It took me a quarter of an hour to travel a few hundred yards through the white water and past an inner bar. Although the waves were widely spaced, each had enough power to send you back as far as you could paddle before the next arrived. I had to roll off my battered rented board and dive for the bottom when I arrived at the bar at the same time as a set, and hope that it withstood the pounding. Its leash, meanwhile, dragged on my bad leg, twisting and tugging like a demented and malevolent physiotherapist.

As ever in Famara, the view from the sea was beautiful. It had rained overnight and mist hung down the flanks of Los Riscos, so that they resembled those of a Scottish glen, and one might have mistaken the distant cacti for bracken and the darker goats for deer. Although the sky was overcast, the water was luminous – sometimes jade green, sometimes viridian. The waves were bigger and slower than they had been at San Juan, with great thick lips that shoved rather than punched. Manuel had advised that it was important to take off on them at an angle to the left or right, rather than go straight and bottom turn immediately as had been the case on the reef. I lined up, paddled hard, popped up on my board and was jolted with pain from my hip at a critical instant. I teetered for a second but made the take-off and the thrill of accelerating blanked out the agony. I was transfixed as the water in front of me spun up from a flat sea to form the wave that I was riding. We're programmed for travelling over terra firma rather than fluid, and the sight of the ground beneath your feet streaming skywards is disconcertingly counter-intuitive. Sometimes beginners scrabble at it with their arms from an ingrained desire to get a purchase. We may fly in our dreams but in real life we fall: cling on to the edge if you can.

My rides were good but each was more painful than the last, until despite the brain saying yes, the body said no. I'd tell myself to spring up, and find the command had failed. Perhaps such decisions are too important to be left to the rational mind, which might hum and haw and even take a perverse pleasure in pain. But our memories of pain are animal as well as conscious, and hold us back, even when we've forgotten how much it hurts when we're injured. The instinct for self-preservation takes over and steers us to safety, sometimes against our will. I gave up and rode in to the beach on my knees.

That evening I limped out for a beer at Café Sol, the only bar in the village with a terrace by the sea. It was full and my fellow customers were all of an age. Every male head was white, silver or bald. The ladies favoured metallic tints of purple and bronze. The last of the day's sunlight hit their faces at a narrow angle, etching shadows into their wrinkles and highlighting their whiskers. Their conversations were both animated and decorous. Life – what was left of it – was sweet. Like me, they'd come to Lanzarote to try to stave off old age, albeit they were travelling a little closer to the curl.

Manuel passed by with a friend and asked, 'How's your hip?'

'Not good,' I told him. 'It feels like bone on bone.'

'Bones hurt,' he said, and grinned. 'When I cracked a vertebra last year…'

'You broke your back surfing?'

'Not badly, and only once.'

I felt like a fraud, and was ashamed that I'd looked for sympathy when none was deserved. Manuel introduced his friend, Alonso, who was sailing for Antigua from Gran Canaria that Sunday. I told him I'd made almost the same journey seventeen years before.

'Any thoughts?' he asked.

I thought: how had it gone after that first wild night downwind? I remembered that we'd under-provisioned and arrived in St Lucia with only a single onion left to eat between six of us; and that we'd split the main sail, and hadn't sailed far enough south and so had been becalmed for two days.

'Go south,' I told him, 'until the clouds change. The trade wind clouds are easy to spot – they look like they've been panted out by steam trains. And don't turn west too early lest the wind die in your sails.'

SANDWICH ISLANDERS PLAYING IN THE SURF

16
Line-Ups

December 2016

I'd picked up floaters in Lanzarote. If I turned my head
suddenly, a swarm of little black bees would zoom around
the edges of my vision, then scoot away into nothingness
when I tried to follow their paths. They were disconcerting
when they first appeared, but have since become my
familiars as they dance among the fairy lights and other
Christmas decorations. Floaters are caused by tiny lumps of
debris that drift about the jelly inside our eyeballs, casting
shadows on our retinas. They result from general wear and
tear – or from being fire-hosed with salt water. They can
cause their owners serious mental problems if they don't
know what they are. My friend Fred once told me about
his uncle who suffered from them and thought he could
see small shaggy creatures scampering around the room
whenever he sat down. 'There's a good one!' he'd shout,
and point at an empty space and laugh. His relatives
thought he was insane, and over time he came to accept

their judgement, embellishing his floaters with names, and even characters.

My Christmas present to myself had arrived when I was in the Canaries. It was the ghost of Christmases past: a Tokoro mini-gun, shaped for surfing fast, hollow waves. It came in a coffin-shaped cardboard box. The board was brand new and powder-blue, and looked like a toothpick in comparison to the slug-shaped rental board I'd used in Lanzarote. Long, slim and pointed, as if it had been pared to its essence, the Tokoro's shape resembled a double-edged stabbing spear. It was – perversely – designed to be slow. When waves are big and fast, control counts for more than out-and-out speed. Although a wide tail on a surfboard is a fast tail, its edges can snag – with catastrophic consequences if you're riding six Hawaiian feet. Hence my new board had a rounded pin tail and was scarcely a foot wide across above its fins. I admired its beauty in the abstract, as I knew I wouldn't be able to use it now, if ever. Its dimensions – $6'8" \times 18'\frac{1}{4}" \times 2'\frac{1}{4}"$ – were inked onto its stringer, together with the message 'Jesus Loves You!'

Amen. I needed a touch of the Holy Stoke. I'd bought the Tokoro to be my tube board. But one needed the grace and balance of a panther to ride it at all, and I was crippled. Sometimes it was less painful to hop than limp and I spent much of Christmas on one leg.

I'd had more bad news from the doctor – a specialist had examined my X-ray and had spotted deterioration that the radiologist had missed. Short of a miracle, I'd need another hip operation. Although the news was depressing, it wasn't as frightening as it had been first time around, in the sense that I expected to live through it rather than haemorrhaging under the knife or succumbing to toxic shock upon the first contact with bone cement. The anaesthetic, of course, might paralyse me for life, but presumably I would be compensated with millions and would then be able to afford a custom surf canoe and helpers to rescue me if I wiped out. My greater fear was of being sent back to the beginning of my quest and having to start all over again – hobbling up and down hills, re-mastering the wobble board, leaning and falling instead of leaning and turning. Next time, the temptation to refuse the challenge might be too strong. I might give in, sign up to Sky TV, start following football, invest in a pipe and a pair of fleecy slippers, and hone my stories of what might have been.

My nephews Ralf and Channing came to stay over the holidays and were keen to surf with me and Will, my stepson. The swell was good and forecast to continue that way, and to refuse them would have been to admit failure. We settled on a mission to Bantham in a couple of days, which bought me time to either obtain some horse tranquilizers for the session or dream up an excuse for not getting in the water. To whet our appetites for the real thing, Will dug out some of the surf videos we used to watch together when he and Ralf and Channing were in their early teens and still all shorter than me. It was a stroke of genius. First up was *Crystal Voyager*, a film I'd first seen as a schoolboy in 1975, which opens with footage shot from the insides of waves as they closed into tubes, and the lines:

> You might be in there for only seconds in real time, but in your head, it goes on for hours. It's an experience that's hard to describe – riding inside the eye of a big, grinding wave. Often, you're riding so deep inside the tube you don't make it out. You take a terrible wipeout. But what matters is when you're in there. It's a time warp when you're inside the wave. Time enters a space, a zone of its own. The only reality is what's happening right then.

I'd forgotten that *Crystal Voyager* had introduced me to the cult of the tube. It's a documentary which follows a surfer named George Greenough as he builds boards and boats, and voyages up and down the Californian coast in search of clean, empty waves. Greenough rides a kneeboard in most of the movie as he flies around inside tubes and shoots up and down the faces of blue-green Pacific swells, performing turns tighter than any upright surfer of that era could manage. Apart from the surfing the film is slow-paced and beautifully self-indulgent. Its ultimate twenty-three minutes, shot by Greenough with a heavy film camera on his back, consist of underwater and surface footage of tubes, with waves spinning into the sky, foam melding with clouds, at times reminiscent of images of supernovas, at others the journey from a womb into daylight; accompanied by the full version of Pink Floyd's 'Echoes'.

The movie had mystified me when I saw it on a winter's night in London, on exeat from boarding school. It offered a window into a world so different from the grimy rainy city outside the cinema, and the prison camp in the country where I had to return the next day, that it had lodged itself in my memory and perhaps had sown the seed of my desire, one day, to ride a tube. Watching it forty-three years later, it once again served as inspiration: if I couldn't catch one on my feet, I might yet succeed on my knees.

Kneeboarding is an esoteric style of surfing that sits in a category of its own. It's acknowledged as inspiring the revolution in board design that occurred around the time that *Crystal Voyager* was released, and George Greenough's performance in the film has been described as 'nothing less than a blueprint for shortboard surfing'. Kneeboarding also has an ancient pedigree: engravings of Polynesians show them surfing on their knees as well as riding upright. And St Piran – it may be presumed – rode his millstone into Cornwall kneeling in prayer, rather than strutting up to its edge and hanging ten. It is, however, a dying art – at least in Britain.

When I looked for kneeboard surfboards for sale online, I felt like an anthropologist sent to study a foreign civilization who arrives full of hope, only to discover that it has recently moved on, leaving little more that abandoned huts with cold ashes in their hearths. The internet was full of dead ends – threads that ran, say, from 2008 to 2012 then stopped abruptly. It was as if all the kneeboarders over here had expired, or given up and moved inland, within the space of a few years. After hunting high and low and drawing blanks everywhere – eBay, Gumtree, Magicseaweed and various shapers' pages, I struck gold. A call to Triocean Surf, a few miles away from Bantham, revealed that they had not one but two kneeboards for sale, both, they said, in execrable condition. Neither was watertight – one, a quad fish from Byron Bay in New South Wales, had a cracked nose and a gouge out of one rail; the other, shaped in Cornwall by Chris Diplock, had holes in the deck and a dinged tail. But the Diplock board could be patched up sufficiently to take out for a few sessions. My hands were shaking with excitement when I hung up.

Whilst idealists such as Mexican revolutionary Emiliano Zapata, who claimed 'I would rather die on my feet than live on my knees',* might have baulked at surfing kneeling, I had no such qualms and would have countered his objections with his own words: 'I want to die a slave to principles, not to men.' I wanted to ride a tube and if people who surfed badly on their feet looked down on kneeboarding, then I was above their disdain. After watching a few videos of Hawaiian kneeboarders airdropping into Pipeline, and Australians charging G-land in Java, I was satisfied that it was no compromise. It seems that kneeboarding had fallen out of favour because it had been squeezed between the advances in shortboard board design it had inspired

---

* 'Prefiero morir de pie que vivir de rodillas.'

– which enabled shortboarders to turn at first equally and then more quickly on waves – and bodyboarding, whose tribe could ride even smaller, tighter, faster breaks; rather than having been left behind in the evolutionary strata of surfing. Besides, it harked back to an age when time spent on one's knees was considered meritorious and a way of hastening one's admission to heaven.

I couldn't wait to start.

January 2017

I had my first proper kneeboard session at Saunton Sands in North Devon. Saunton was described by my pocket guide to surf in southwest England as a 'gutless' break, albeit with space enough to accommodate hundreds of losers. Its only stated hazards were the strong rip currents that appeared when it was above six feet, and its tides.* The beach runs for several miles between a rocky headland to the north and the estuary of the River Taw to the south. Like Woolacombe, it's vast when the tide is out, and long and narrow when it's in. When I got there the swell was beautifully spaced and chest-high to overhead. The view out to sea was coloured sepia: grey sets with clear crests, backlit by a faded red winter sun.

My new kneeboard was too wide to fit under my arm, so

---

* Its spring tides have a range of ten metres and peak flows that would wash even the strongest swimmers sideways.

I carried it on my head down to the sands. It was no beauty, although not quite as battered as it had been described over the phone. A couple of lumps of Session Saver putty had made it watertight, its rails were clean, and the finer points of its design still shone through the dings and creases. When I laid it down to do my stretches I was struck by its difference from my other surfboards. It was like meeting an old friend who'd suddenly become fat instead of merely rounded. It was as broad as the Mini Simmons, but a foot shorter, with its fins placed a long way up the board from its tail. Rather than scribbled circles of wax, it had rubber pads on its face – prayer mats – showing me where to kneel.

I paddled out at the northern end of Saunton, which is known as 'longboarders' corner', where the waves well up in such a way that longboarders can catch them twenty yards further out than shortboarders, and so cream off most of the best rides. I chose it because if a big set came through, its faces would be too steep for them, and kneeboards were said to be the best for late take-offs.

The peak had the oldest average age of surfer that I'd ever come across. Although people were pinched by the cold air and water, which add years and wrinkles to all but the most youthful of faces, and even manage to age teenagers – turning their pink cheeks purple like a drunk's – there were men and women out there who must have been in their sixties. One crabbed figure on an SUP leant on his paddle as if it was a crutch and had the skin and veins of an eighty-year-old. It was a glimpse into the kind of future

I was planning for myself – to keep surfing right on into the twilight zone.

I spent quarter of an hour giving way to veterans, who always seemed to be in the right place at the right time when a set came through, until they'd all caught rides and I arrived at the front of the rank. I turned, paddled hard, got planing, popped up onto my knees, and started to stand when I remembered I was already in position. It took me a couple more waves to get over the 'is that it?' – of being what seemed only halfway up – then it was fun all the way, outrageous fun, such as I hadn't felt for years. It took me back to my pre hip-op days of surfing without tears, when every ride had been a blast. I whizzed along waves, turned by looking and leaning, and stroked their faces as I passed across them. And it was easy – blissfully easy – I hadn't realized how much I'd been held back by pain over the last few months.

I stayed out until my muscles turned to jelly, then caught a last wave right into the beach and rolled off my board in ankle-deep water.

My right leg ached as I drove home. I'd made the mistake of sitting astride the board when I was waiting for waves, forcing my injured bones together. I was, however, in a mood to celebrate my rebirth as a kneeboarder, so poured myself a tumbler of port from a bottle we'd somehow missed over Christmas, which buoyed up my happiness and numbed a little of the pain. We had friends round to dinner that night and one of them, Jim, spoke about alternative cures, even for cancer – of tumours vanishing overnight when crystals were placed next to them. When I told him that I would be happy to paint myself bright pink and wear peacock feathers in my hair if it might cure my hip, he took me seriously. Pink, he said, was a good idea, as rose quartz was the best therapeutic stone for arthritis – though my intuition had failed me when it came to feathers, which he said were used to heal people who'd suffered strokes.

Whereas in 2014 I'd turned my back on quackery and the faint chance that it might regenerate lost cartilage and damaged bone, this time I was ready to embrace it. After our guests had left, I spent over a hundred pounds on Amazon within a couple of minutes buying healing gels, soothing sprays and a magnetized copper bracelet. Next stop, Holland & Barrett where a similar amount vanished on micronutrient supplements. At times, I had to close my eyes to the evidently mendacious publicity that appeared alongside some of the branded joint-care products that I added to my shopping basket, which peddled false hopes to people in pain. I wasn't yet ready to believe that 500 mg of glucosamine, which has been proven in trial after clinical trial to offer no benefits whatsoever to victims of arthritis, or an even smaller amount of 'pharma-grade' collagen, of which there was already plenty in my diet, might let me dance the twist again.

While I waited – with an open mind – for these elixirs to start working, I caught a few more sessions on my kneeboard.

Each was as good as the first. Although I hadn't yet learned the art of leaving a wave gracefully, I hadn't fallen off one once and was surfing as well as I ever had. My joy was only constrained by the cold. A fortnight of frosts and icy offshore winds numbed my skin and dulled my senses when I was out on the water. Every time I duck dived through a wave I felt like I'd been slapped in the face, and it seemed to take forever to stop gasping, catch my breath and get into position for the next set. Above all the cold was tiring. Shivering took up as much energy as surfing and after an hour and a half in the sea I was usually worn out. I was happy though and developed an appetite that bordered on the savage. The front of my car was filled with empty pie boxes and pasty wrappers as I gorged my way home after every surf.

I was flying by wire on my initial kneeboard sessions, leaning and turning by instinct rather than trying to follow steps in manoeuvres that I'd been taught. When a storm blew in and the waves blew out, I searched online to see if I could find any guides or tips for self-improvement: should I have my knees together or apart? Salaam vigorously to get the board pumping? Should I continue to lean out and touch the face of the wave as I turned, or stay upright with arms crossed? My questions went unanswered. There were thousands of online tutorials telling you how to ride longboards and shortboards, but nothing about knee-boarding techniques. I did, however, discover that it still flourished in pockets around the world. Tim emailed to tell me that there were kneeboard-shapers and surf shops in Byron Bay, and that George Greenough was alive and well, living nearby in a glass pyramid in the rainforest behind Broken Head, surfing on air mattresses and filming dolphins. He met him sometimes on the beach.

Miles, meanwhile, advised that Cantabria, just up the coast from Galicia, was awash with kneeboarders – perhaps because it had smaller tubes. He even knew one, Ramon, who'd told him to tell me that I'd get my best rides on shallow rock reefs. The name and the hint stirred a memory. One of the few surfers I knew in Bridport, Roman from Uruguay, had told me about a reef break down the coast from us that had good waves but horrendous crowds, and had showed me a picture of it on his phone.

Horrible, he said, horrible, and stabbed at the screen with his forefinger, as if he was trying to squash something on it. Apparently in Uruguay if there's already a surfer in the water, you go somewhere else. I was about to ask him where the crowds were in the photo, as I'd been so taken by the swells it pictured that I'd eyes for little else, when Roman switched off his phone and shoved it the hip pocket of his jeans. Kimmeridge, he told me, was *terminado*, *perdido* – finished, lost.

February 2017

From the air, Kimmeridge looks like a shark has taken a bite out of the cliffs just west of Swanage. Its crescent bay holds patches of flat Jurassic reef within its arms and their tips are bounded by stone ledges. It's located inside the perimeter of an army firing range and surfing is forbidden on one of its breaks when the guns are aiming out to sea. The bay is backed by pocket handkerchief fields and hollows, sprinkled with cottages and copses, and is edged by low cliffs whose coloured strata overhang its clear blue waters. It's as pretty as a postcard.

Kimmeridge is believed by New Agers to be imbued with special powers. Their speculations may be supported by objective as well as subjective evidence, for it seems to have been a magnet for creators and dreamers for several thousand years. It was inhabited during the Iron Age by an unknown culture, who used compasses and lathes to shape and cut bracelets from the jet-black shale that forms one of the layers of strata in its cliffs. These have been found as far away as Switzerland, suggesting that they had a value – probably sacred rather than aesthetic, for while the local rock looks appealing enough when polished up, it scuffs easily and doesn't keep its lustre for long. The next culture to inhabit Kimmeridge left charms, amulets and the remains of a bull that they'd sacrificed then buried at a point overlooking the sea. The discovery of its remains in the nineteenth century caused both excitement and controversy amongst antiquarians, some of whom took it as proof that the bay had once been a Phoenician settlement, whilst others believed it showed that a cult worshipping Neptune, tended by priestesses called *Maritimes*, had flourished there in Roman times.

The bull was dug up by shale miners. One of the thickest layers in Kimmeridge's multitude of strata is oil shale, which burns like coal, and this drew merchant adventurers to it in the sixteenth and seventeenth centuries who hoped to make their fortunes by mining the shale, or using it for fuel to boil seawater into salt. Sir William Clavell built an alum works by the bay, only to fall foul of a Jacobean monopoly on its production, and 'the Farmers of the Allom Works' seized his equipment and stole his cattle. Clavell's descendants next attempted to establish salt distilleries and glass manufactories at Kimmeridge, but none lasted. Five hundred years of stillborn industrial revolutions lie under its soil. Its cliffs are honeycombed with mine shafts and tunnels, and decorated with relics from these as well as amulets and the usual fossils. A pair of tangled railway lines hang out of the cliff face just inside the eastern arm of the bay, and next to these a wagon on cast-iron wheels is emerging from the stones.

Ness and I had gone to Kimmeridge on a joint expedition – she to look for driftwood to use in her art and me for waves. We parked the car at the top of the cliffs and both enthused over the view. Long period swell was rolling into the bay, peeling off its reefs and round the points of both its arms. The shore was cluttered with promising-looking flotsam. She dashed off with the dogs, I suited up and walked down the stairs on the coastal path to the beach. Halfway down there was a hinged metal notice board, painted red, which permitted or prohibited access when opened or shut. It was padlocked shut and read:

RANGE WALKS ARE CLOSED

BROAD BENCH IS CLOSED FOR SURFING

FIRING IN PROGRESS

I didn't know which of the peaks was Broad Bench so hurried down the remaining steps and got straight into the sea. The water at Kimmeridge was far clearer than my usual breaks on the Dorset coast and was coloured Prussian-blue, with foam as white as egret feathers, rather than the customary café au lait with chocolate-brown clots in its spume. The tide was rising, and as I paddled some of the breaks I'd seen from the top of the cliff became covered with too much water and stopped working, so I headed at the tip of the eastern arm of the bay, towards a peak that was still standing tall.

It was the best break I'd seen since San Juan in Lanzarote. It was a long paddle out, and I stopped a couple of times on the way just to look at it: steep waves breaking with metronomic regularity, with surfers hitting their lips and firing across their faces, while the sections they'd just ridden collapsed with bone-shaking booms!

Sadly, there was no Manuel behind my ear to tell me how to ride them. I sat on the edge of the break and then out the back, looking and learning. It was left-handed, which was as easy as a right-hander to a kneeboarder, since you face straight forward and don't have a blind side like stand-up surfers do. There were boils on the water when the smaller sets passed without breaking, indicating rocks below. As in

Lanzarote, I'd have to take off pointing at shore then turn sharply, rather than trying to tuck in straight away and risk getting tumbled onto the reef.

A current was running east with the tide, and I searched for line-ups on land so as to know where I was in relation to the place where the waves were breaking. Your sense of perspective is so limited when you're surfing that the best way of judging where you are on the sea is by aligning features on the shore. Choose one close to the water and one behind it, and if the near one starts travelling to the right, paddle left and vice versa. Ideally you should find three markers so that you can triangulate your position fore and aft as well as sideways. Line-ups may be picturesque or mundane according to your location. Whereas in Java, you might align a coconut tree with the peak of a distant volcano, in Devon it's more likely to be a stunted palm against the façade of a fish-and-chip kiosk, with the toilet block of a caravan park the third point of reference.

The line-ups at Kimmeridge were scenic. In 1830, one of its failed industrialists built the Clavell Tower, a tubular folly in the Tuscan style, on the headland above the surf, which, together with a stripe on the cliff below, serves as a reference point in the lateral plane. Meanwhile, how near to or far away you are from shore can be determined by marking the position of the nodding donkey, pumping oil out of a well on the point above the eastern corner of the bay. If there's sea behind the donkey, you're too close.

It took me a long time to catch a wave. Although they

were cantering rather than charging, I kept getting left behind. I was trapped inside by a larger set and had to slide off my board and kick out for the bottom when one detonated over my head. I could feel the shock wave in my body as it travelled through the water and bounced off the reef. I think this deafened me, as my memories of the rest of the session are silent.

I air-dropped into my first wave, taking off so late that I fell from its crest to its base while perched on the tail of my board, expecting to part company with it at any instant. But I made my bottom turn and shot along the wave as it walled up behind my left shoulder. I bailed out when I could see the reef through the surface – a mess of brown and purple blotches, swirling with seaweed. Although the water was blue it was cloudy, and so much visible detail meant that it was only a couple of feet deep. I noticed a surfer without a board on the way back out – just a head sticking out of the sea. As I paddled over the head turned, a body rolled with a glimpse of fins: it was a seal.

I caught a couple more waves in my silent session. Another surfer spoke to me – I remember his mouth opening and closing but not his words. He had red-blond hair and beard and very even features, and reminded me of a figure on a cigarette card – a stylized mariner. He knew the break well, so I stayed close and was rewarded with my best ride of the day by paddling into the slot he'd just vacated. It broke at a very narrow angle to shore so that I had to turn, cut back, and turn in quick succession to stay with the shoulder. Although it was done without style I was pleased with myself that I'd managed it at all – this was how I had hoped I would have been surfing in Lanzarote.

When I came off the wave I saw Ness on shore, a tall slim figure with long blonde hair, striding over the rocks, looking out to sea. I waved, she waved back, and pointed at a collection of cars on the point. She'd moved ours down from the cliffs. I paddled round and found a slipway, coated in emerald slime, which I crept up on all fours, pushing my board in front of me until I ran out of water, grateful that I hadn't had to stumble out over the rocks. Ness met me by the car.

'Did you hear the guns?' she asked.

I hadn't.

'I saw a seal,' I told her.

'So did I,' said Ness. 'There's a dead one in the rocks, covered in flies. The dogs rolled in it.'

I noticed the patches of matted fur on their backs. They seemed very pleased with themselves: their heads were up, their ears pricked and they wagged their tails with extra vigour. Perhaps they were waiting for me to savour the rich and rare aromas of rotting flesh and fat with which they'd robed themselves, and share their elation. We kept the car windows open for the journey home.

17
Close-Outs

March 2017

Kimmeridge had been a step up. If I could surf a wave like that with a reasonable degree of confidence, then I was ready for more demanding breaks. I could focus on how to catch a tube, rather than how to ride a wave. I emailed Tim in Australia to ask for tips and he answered that I had to be fast, which I read as meaning he'd offer more advice when I could say, with my hand on my heart, that I was fast enough. I called Marcus, the only other kneeboarder I knew, who'd ridden tubes in Britain, France and Ireland, and he said he'd learned to hold his breath underwater for two minutes before he'd cut his teeth at the reef break off Porthleven. I also spoke to Eamon, an ex-bodyboarder, who'd spent more time getting tubed than most stand-up surfers.

'Start with close-outs,' he told me.

A close-out is a wave that collapses along its entire length as it breaks rather than peeling either to the left or right, like a line of falling cards. Close-outs are unsurfable. Waves can also close out in sections while you're riding them, and the sense of betrayal is overwhelming: you struggle to catch one, pop up, aim down the line, whereupon the face turns over itself, buries you in white water and tumbles you away from the break. When this happens, it's easy to anthropomorphize individual waves and characterize them as malicious, born only to destroy your happiness. And these were the kind that Eamon was advising me to seek out. The idea, apparently, was to gain experience of being inside a tube, albeit one without an exit. And since things would go wrong, you could learn about them one by one and, sometimes, how to deal with them.

Tim's advice made the most sense. I needed to speed up my surfing: take off quicker, make sharper turns and cut back quick as a lightning bolt, on my knees. Being rolled up in close-outs could wait until I was worthy of them. The best way to hone my reflexes would be to ride small, fast waves where I would need to react quickly and could also catch plenty of them. I might have to enter bodyboarder territory to find them.

Bodyboarders are the *enfants terribles* of wave riding. They take pride in charging breaks no upright surfer would attempt. Although they kneel, and even stand on their boards, as well as riding them on their bellies, they are considered a caste of untouchables by longboarders, who would rather kiss a leper than shake one by the hand. This antipathy derives from the fact that 'boogers' can steal waves from longboarders at ease, and rob them of the same advantage they enjoy, and exploit without qualms, over shortboarders and kneeboarders. Bodyboarders use swim fins to generate speed at take off and are famed for the diameters of their calves rather than the soundness of their bottoms. Their fins also provoke the ire of loggers, who deem them sacrilegious, on the grounds that they are an artificial means of propulsion: if you're going to strap on fins, then stop pretending to surf and buy a motorboat.

I checked the bodyboarders' territory online, searching in their argot with key words and phrases such as 'sponger', 'booger', 'drop knee' and 'brass neck'. It was surprisingly barren. They seemed to have lost interest in the virtual world a few years after kneeboarders. Most of their forums had petered out by 2014. I was surprised: I'd expected them to be garrulous amongst themselves, and had hoped to eavesdrop on them. Had they pushed their riding so far that too many broke their backs? Had a shadow fallen over serious bodyboarding, as opposed to the holiday variety, practised at the water's edge?

On reflection, I realized they were similar to all other surfers, including shortboarders and longboarders, who also had a limited presence online. The top surfing website generates seventy times less traffic, in terms of visitors per month, than its equivalent for golfers; and surfers are all but invisible – a drop in the ocean – against the hundreds of millions visiting gaming, gambling, dating and body-

building sites, and the billions who click on YouTube.*
I've never considered myself screen shy, but it seems that
the hundred or so hours I spend each year looking at the
swell charts and webcams on surf pages is a minor fixation
compared to the thousands of hours logged up by a lonely
video gamer on steroids.

My research yielded a few clues as to suitable spots: there
was a wedge at Tolcarne, a reef near Seaton, and a ledge at
Challaborough. All were subject to the usual vagaries of
swell, wind and tide. Tolcarne was the most reliable but a
long drive away in west Cornwall, and only fired at high
water. Seaton, just over the county border in Devon, needed
at least seven feet of long-period groundswell from 210°
and wind from the northwest quadrant of the compass. It
was the closest but the last two miles to the break were on
foot, down a steep coast path with occasional near-vertical
sections where you had to lower your board by its leash,
climb down the cliff to it, and repeat, before jumping in
off the rocks at the end of the point, and my hip wasn't
up to it. Challaborough, round the coast from Bigbury,
looked to be the best option. It had a right-hand point
break over stone and sand, which worked when the swell

---

* Whose viewing numbers are phenomenal. 'Shake it Off' by Taylor
  Swift has been watched nearly two and a half billion times. Even
  if it is assumed that every one of its viewers has seen it four times,
  more people have gawked over the Canadian chanteuse than the
  total number of native English speakers in the world, and a further
  multiple of those who know, or knew, who Shakespeare was.

was anywhere between west and south and was best at mid-tide.

I passed back and forth between seasons on my drive to Challaborough. There were pockets in the landscape where winter still ruled, where the woods were bare and brown, then the road would twist to the south and the Blackthorn would be misted with blossom and the verges decorated with primroses. The wind through the car windows smelled of regeneration, of new life bursting out of the ground. The sky clouded over after I passed Exeter and I drove through a series of thunderstorms. The rain was torrential – heavier than the wipers could clear. This, combined with the walls of spray thrown up from the vehicles I overtook in the inside lane, and the saturated surface of the road, rendered the view through the windscreen aquatic and reminiscent of a scene from *Crystal Voyager*, played in fast forward.

When I got close to the coast I decided to look in on Bantham before Challaborough. A six-foot swell was forecast to arrive there that afternoon from the Atlantic and it merited a short detour. The bearded retainer at the gate to its car park was a new man in the rain. I was listening to a programme on the car radio about how the Victorians had invented everything and he weighed in with some knowledgeable asides while I fished around for change to buy my ticket. At that point, I realized he was a different individual from the one who'd scowled for England on my last visit – same job, different beards – and that this one, in addition to his sunny character, had tattoos on his arms of motorbikes and raven-haired girls dressed in leather and lace. We parted on the best of terms and he offered me a cup of tea in his booth on my way out.

Bantham was good – too good to trade for an unknown ledge at Challaborough, which may, for all I knew, be closing out. The waves were overhead and spaced a long way apart. It was a proper groundswell, born in a storm over a thousand miles away. I changed as quickly as I could, munched some painkillers, skipped my stretches and paddled out. I was riding a new board for the first time, which I'd bought the week before, when I'd spotted it online at a bargain price. My Diplock board had so many dings and creases it might break without warning, so I struck a deal and met the new board's maker, Bryn, on a council estate in Plymouth for the handover. He was small and neat, with bright-blue eyes, and pulled it out of its bag with a flourish for me to admire. I could see it was great, but was eager for tips on how to ride it rather than wanting its rails explained, section by section, from nose to tail.

Spread your knees, he told me, sit back when you turn, and stay low on the wave and push your weight forward when you're getting tubed. And that, apparently, was it. All the rest was detail. I started to count out its price in cash, but Bryn stopped me and said I'm sure it's fine. He explained that our place of rendezvous was popular with drug dealers who might suspect us of invading their turf, take the money and the board – and then set their pit bulls on us.

My first wave at Bantham on the new board was a beauty: a left-hander, it went on and on as I dropped to its base, returned to its face and carved round a close-out section. I was so rapt I stayed with it right into the river mouth, until it crossed a deep channel and left me behind. The tide was rising and I had to paddle hard against the flood to avoid getting washed up the Avon, then even harder out through the white water past a sandbar where the smaller sets were breaking. Although the new board paddled well for its length, it was only 5'8" and required effort to get moving. It likewise needed plenty of shove to duck dive. I forced myself to keep my eyes open when I went under, so as to be sure that I'd pushed the nose down deep enough. The board was too wide to sit astride with any comfort, and when I reached the break I slipped off, turned it sideways and propped myself up across it on my elbows, as if it was the counter of a bar.

There were five- to ten-minute gaps between the taller sets. Only a handful of other surfers had the patience to wait for them, a hundred yards further out from where the rest of the waves rolled over. The rainstorms had passed and an icy breeze blew off the land. Those with bare hands buried them under their armpits and sat hunched forwards, their chins against their chests. Some, whose faces were the colour of raw mince, clearly had been out for hours. No one spoke. Their postures reminded me of the peasants in a Pieter Bruegel painting, albeit truncated at the waist, huddled against the cold in a wintry landscape.

Everyone became animated when a set approached. Their heads went up, they uncrossed their arms, spun on their boards and started paddling. We all looked at each other as well as the waves, trying to judge who had right of way and whether or not the person who did would catch them or waste them. Meanwhile the lines arriving from the sea glittered at their crests before rearing and falling. I couldn't paddle as fast as my competitors and had to take off late, when their lips curled over their bases, and air-drop onto their faces. An air-drop is when you fall through the air at take-off, rather than retaining contact with the wave. Although the drop at Bantham was only five feet, it felt like a far greater distance in my state of accelerated consciousness. As soon as I touched down I had to twist left or right and slip a rail into the wave to generate lift and speed.

I found I was starting far lower on the wave than usual. The water on the face of a breaker is travelling upwards as well as forwards, and the upward force seemed more pronounced at its base. I hadn't been on this part of a wave very often before, and then not for years, and I felt disorientated, as though I'd woken up in a strange room or entered a new state of mind. The world seemed taller and narrower – tucked in and pulled up – as if, like the wave, it was streaming towards the sky.

I caught some close-outs after all. The peak shifted as the tide rose and the last section of its right-handers now broke along a bar that ran parallel to the beach. The section ahead of me on the wave that I was riding changed colour suddenly from green to brown as it sucked sand off the seabed. The next instant my board shot up sideways and set me spinning as the wave thumped down on me. The force was terrific. It blasted the air out of my lungs, then tumbled me along the bottom in a vortex of foam and grit. When I surfaced, gasping and quaking, a bodyboarder a dozen yards or so down the line, in his thirties, with a bull neck and shaven head, gave me the thumbs-up and a jealous smile, pinched at its edges – perhaps it was just the cold.

I fell into the same trap on my next ride and came up aching all over. We may be seven-tenths water, but we are also bones. I was ready to go in and then an all-but-forgotten phrase popped into my head: one more wave.

This is a mantra amongst surfers. Even when you're dog-tired and the waves are getting harder and harder to catch, if the rides have been flowing you never want to go in. The memory of pleasure outweighs present pain. Just one more wave before night falls, you say to yourself, one good one that will give me joy and take me right into shore. The mantra has special resonance when you're over the hill: catch them while you can. I settled for a left-hander on the inside bank, which peeled instead of slamming shut. When it finally broke under me I rode its white-water ghost into the shallows on my belly.

My drive home shone. The sense that I'd been to a new country persisted; the new board had been a revelation and my pair of close-outs quickly mutated in the memory from deeply unpleasant into interesting experiences. I found I was leaning with the curves, as if still riding waves, when I navigated the twisting country lanes out of Bantham.

I had a few more good days on my new board and felt confident enough to email Tim in Australia again and ask him, what came after speed?

He was well, he replied, his family were well too, and the swell had been firing, although the man in the grey suit* had paid a visit to Wategos Bay, and those who wished to stay out of the food chain were doing DIY until the great white that had killed a surfer there had been caught. I'd surfed Wategos with Tim, Bunny and Kyle in February 2005, and remembered it for the beauty of its water. When I looked straight down through the sea as I waited for a wave it was as clear as spring water, but if I shifted my head even slightly, planes and patches of topaz, aquamarine and carnelian would appear, fluttering and melting on its surface and in its depths. When a set arrived and the waves began to pitch, the sea spun itself into rainbows and foam.

As for tubes, Tim concluded, remember to keep your eyes open.

Open for what? Sharks? Rocks? Crowds? Or was he alluding to the tendency of people who are in a state of panic

---

* A shark.

to screw their eyes tight shut, revert to childhood and believe that if they closed their eyes they would become invisible and whatever was threatening them would let them be? Was Tim suggesting I might panic if I found myself in a tube? I looked up other symptoms of panic attacks beyond denial pure and simple, which included, according to the NHS website, hot flushes, chills, hearing a ringing sound in your ears, a 'feeling of dread or a fear of dying', and 'a need to go to the toilet'. Whilst I'd experienced hot flushes during a strenuous bout of paddling, chills after diving through a winter wave, and ringing ears following a wipeout, premonitions of death or a weak sphincter had yet to trouble my surfing sessions. I felt confident that I would keep my eyes open, emailed Tim the news, and he replied great – go for it, and asked, did I have a break in mind?

I did: Croyde in Devon, sandwiched between Saunton and Woolacombe. In contrast to its neighbours to the north and south, whose beaches stretch for miles, Croyde is a narrow bay with stone jaws and a tongue of sand poking out the middle. The jaws reach out to funnel the waves in, and the sets there are bigger, faster and hollower than any-where else on that stretch of Devon's coast. Croyde has a couple of A-frame peaks, where waves break left and right simultaneously from a single point like the apex of a capital A, and another over the rocks on its northern edge. All three form tubes in the right conditions. Croyde also has a reputation as a board snapper, and I'd avoided it before for that very reason, together with rumours that it was packed with locals who spoke Devonish patois and dropped in on strangers they deemed to be unworthy of their waves. I'd driven past it when visiting Woolacombe a few months back and pulled over at a layby where tourists park to eat their chips and gaze at the sea. The waves had been too big, too grey under the low clouds hanging over the landscape, and altogether too challenging. I wondered, if I could dial them up in memory, how they would seem now? Could I ride them?

The question went unanswered for a fortnight as the swell dwindled in the southwest. There were no thrills to be had in the sea, so I took Rosy to Crealy Adventure Park where we rode the roller coasters. Her favourite was the Maximus, themed to 'pay homage to the Roman history of Exeter', that featured an 'ancient Roman train station' and a set of carriages mocked up to look like a Victorian steam locomotive, It flew around a banked and looping track and in and out of a tunnel resembling a mine shaft, suggesting that it had been rebranded at some point in its life. The G-forces that it generated were sufficient to make Rosy scream and me smile, and after our second turn I bought a photograph of us together on the ride. The print features a Roman gladiator brandishing a sword beside us, and a lion roaring its approval below the carriage in which we're seated. Our faces beam with happiness – expressing the pleasure that we're deriving from being thrilled, or scared. I suppose that the Maximus and similar rides are really peddling adrenaline highs. They offer a narrow sort of stimulation that allows us to feel we are facing danger, and so inspire us to release a blast of the hormone from the comfort of a padded seat. A memorable name and the odd plastic legionary are only window dressing.

April 2017

The skies clouded over and the swell returned. The surf forecast sites were unanimous in predicting five- to seven-feet waves with a twelve-second period at Croyde. I checked the webcams, saw it was firing, and drove to North Devon through a cold grey drizzle. The coast road to the beach was closed at Braunton and yellow DIVERSION signs took me through a maze of lanes that coiled around small, steep hills. Spring had taken hold of the landscape and fresh green leaves were unrolling on the trees. Occasional patches of sunshine burst through the clouds, highlighting an orchard in blossom, a thatched cottage by a sparkling stream. I found the scenery frustrating rather than enchanting. My *Wavefinder* guide insisted Croyde was best at low tide – the tide was rising, and I was lost. The lanes meandered round the boundaries of fields rather than proceeding from A to B, so that if I aimed west I was soon travelling north, and when I arrived in the village of Georgeham, which I knew from the map to be just inland of Croyde, it was by accident rather than design. As I inched my way through its streets a tractor emerged from a lane ahead and I had to pull over, fuming with impatience. Even giving way was not enough: I was forced to reverse a dozen yards to a place where the road was wide enough for both of us. I fought to control my scowl when the tractor driver gave me a Devon wave, lifting his thumb and first two fingers from the steering wheel, as though he was offering me a blessing. Then I caught sight of something in my mirror – the stone tower of the village church – which seemed so familiar that I stopped the car, got out and looked at it carefully. It appeared to dwarf the church to which it was attached, and its tiers, buttresses and embattled parapet to belong to a castle rather than a place of worship. I realized I'd been there before but couldn't remember when, or why. As I searched my memory a wooden signpost for the Tarka Trail on the road nearby supplied a clue, and I smiled. It had been in the mid-1980s and I'd been staying with a friend from university – Ben? – at his family's farm, a little further inland from the village. We'd gone out for some pints after dinner and he'd insisted that we made a detour to the church's graveyard, where Tarka's creator Henry Williamson was buried, to pay our respects. I couldn't recall whether the author's grave was marked with a simple head-stone or an elaborate mausoleum, decorated with otters and quotations from his books, but I did remember the church tower in the moonlight.

The realization that I was crossing a path I'd last walked nearly thirty years ago dispelled my frustration and sparked introspection. I imagined meeting myself as I'd been then, on this spot where we'd both stood. I'd turned my back on the sea at the time, had gone hunting and hill walking for recreation, and the existence of a surf beach nearby hadn't even been mentioned by Ben's family, who delighted in country pursuits and would rather have lived at a greater distance from the coast. The view through the eyes of memory is of what one saw rather than how one appeared – a head camera rather than a mirror – and I found I couldn't summon up myself as I was. The best I could manage was a presence rather than a person, raging with energy, topped with dark brown hair, and facing the wrong way.

The clock on the church tower brought me back to the present: time and tide wait for no man. It was already an hour into the flood. I drove on to Croyde with a peaceful mind. Like Georgeham, it was a pretty Devon village with thatched cottages and narrow lanes, but rather than being adorned with flower baskets and fronted with neat hedges, many of the houses on its high street had been converted into surf-cum-souvenir shops that sprouted postcard carousels, rails of wetsuits and racks of boards from their doorways, and had mounds of colourful beach paraphernalia – buckets, shrimp nets, windbreaks and cages full of footballs – laid out on the pavements beside them.

I found a car park after I'd passed through the village and hobbled over the dunes to the beach to look at the sea. I watched the waves for a long time before I suited up and paddled out. They were clean, overhead and very fast. Most of the surfers already in the water were clustered round a peak to the south of the centreline of the beach, which looked just like the pictures I'd seen of Croyde on the web, with waves breaking both ways from its fabled A-frame, just tall enough, as their lips pitched into foam, to cover their riders. The lefts had fewer takers for no other reason, as far as I could judge, than their orientation, which didn't matter to a kneeboarder.

Now I had to work out how to get to them.

I'd brought my Diplock board, which was the quickest one I had but the hardest to duck dive, and didn't want to get mired in the white water on the way out. I studied the surfers riding, falling and returning, so as to lay down a route to the peak in my mind's eye. There were fierce rips swirling along the rocks on either side of the beach and another, less clearly defined, towards its middle, a grey stripe on the lines of foam rolling up the sand. I'd take that one. The wind crept offshore as I watched, drawing lines of spray off the crests.

I felt both apprehensive and excited when I waded into the sea to wait for a gap between sets and follow the course to the break that I'd envisaged. I was nervous only because it looked so wonderful: what great good fortune to be in this place at this time! My elation lasted until I started paddling, whereupon emotion vanished and effort took over. I was puffed out when I reached the peak. A clean-up set had passed through when I was halfway there, and though I'd ducked the first couple of exploding walls that it sent my way, the third caught me and I had to dive for the bottom. When I came up and slipped back on my board, I was snorting salt water out of my nose and my floaters were dancing round my vision. There was barely time to wipe my hair out of my eyes and sprint another twenty yards out to sea when another set arrived. I spun around and went for it.

I took off very late and had to lean back and put my weight on the tail, which stalled the board and slowed it down. I turned parallel to the wave and tucked in a rail. I was low on its face, and saw it dredging sand off the bottom on the section in front, which reared, curled, then pitched over my head. The sheer force of the falling water was astounding and I pressed myself flat against my board as the wave span around me. My principal sensation was one of amazement: in pictures tubes look like veils, a spring morning mist between the surfer and cameraman; in life, this one thundered around me like a river throwing itself over a cliff.

An instant later the barrel collapsed behind me, blasting out the air trapped inside it, which shoved me back into the sunlight, with body shaking and head reeling as I flew on along the wave.

There were faces in the white-water zone ahead, staring up at me. Some were anxious – have you seen me? – terrified that I might ride right over them; others were carefree, oblivious to the figure skimming towards them at high speed – making no attempt at evasive action, as they might have done on land had a wild-eyed stranger come charging at them. I had to wipeout deliberately to prevent a collision.

When I came up, flailing and gasping after being pummelled, I let the foam carry me a little further into shore, until I could stand up amongst the beginners, in the same part of a surf break where I'd started my quest in 2015, now myself one of the fallen angels from the ether beyond.

I didn't catch another wave that day. I reeled in my board by its leash and found it was loose at the tail. The foam had snapped under the fibreglass skin. When I lifted it out of the water, the broken section folded over like a hinge. I stuck it in the back of the car and drove away in a state of disbelief. All the way home I tried to make sense of the experience: I'd just ridden a tube, and had expected that when – if – it happened it would have been marked by what climbers call a 'summit moment' – an instant of clarity, coupled with an overriding sense of achievement such as you might feel when you stand on a mountain peak with clouds alone above, and sketch your route back down the slope beneath your feet to the distant camp you'd left at dawn. But rather than enjoying a sense of fulfilment, I was restless. I felt as if I'd started on a new adventure, rather than completing a quest.

18 April 2017

The swell vanished last week. The days since have been full of sunshine and the nights cold. Surf websites litter their forecasts with the F-word as if it was an expletive: flat, flat, flat! Easter celebrations have kept me distracted in the interim, and when limping round egg hunts palled, I consoled myself with philosophy: Easter commemorates resurrection, the English word *surf* is said to derive from the Latin *surgere*, meaning to arise, and I was ready to grow. I'd learned at Croyde that there was so much more to surfing than I'd yet experienced. The tube had been a window into a new world which had offered a glimpse of fresh pleasures.

My excitement over the opportunities ahead is tempered by the knowledge that I've business pending with a surgeon. I've been referred to a hospital in Southampton for a resurfacing operation on my right hip. With luck, it will come soon. I'll be spared months of degeneration whilst my name creeps up a waiting list and might still be able to paddle out, if there are waves, right up to the day. Meanwhile I'm steeling myself for another stretch as an invalid, when I'll have to suffer condescension as well as pain.

I went to a spring party in the walled garden of an old stone house just after returning from my last session at Bantham. Cocktails were served from trestle tables on its lawn. Canapés were circulated, all good, if a little rich: too much cream on the blinis and in the salmon mousse. The guests were aged between thirty-five and seventy, the majority in their fifties, and were arresting in appearance. It was as if someone had gathered up people at random, aged them playfully or vindictively, made them all overweight by at least two stone, dressed them up in ill-fitting clothing whose colours clashed, and left them to bore each other with platitudes.

Some were solicitous of my limp and asked me what my favourite box set was, as if passive entertainment was all that was left to me in my reduced state. And when I said I'd been surfing that same day, had been out in the sea where the waves had reared above my head, and how I'd flown over their faces, wrapped in the instant, exhilarated and breathless, how I'd been tumbled and spun, how I'd been somewhere they'd never reached, even in their dreams, and told them if they licked their fingers and touched my hair they could taste the salt, I was rewarded with blank, botoxed stares, as if they were waiting until I stopped speaking nonsense, could steer me back to the practicalities of my condition, and talk to me about the best brands of crutches and walking sticks.

When I left the party, I felt that I'd been conferring with ghosts. For all their bulk, its guests had been surprisingly insubstantial presences, as if they were phantoms called forth by the sunlight of these warm spring days, who'd disguised themselves in clothes snatched from washing lines, trying, hoping – but failing – to be alive again.

I wished I'd been able to get through to them, to tell them that even if they thought their active lives were over, they might find, with imagination and endeavour, that they had only just begun. There might be as many years left to them between now and senescence as there were between learning to smile and starting their first jobs. Use them wisely, I wanted to say, and don't die wondering over what might have been. The trick to life is to extract worth from our own insignificance. We know in our hearts that the mountains, woods, and indeed the waves will rise and fall without us. We either need to embrace faith, or embellish these places with stories and turn our actions into a dance, if we wish to make sense out of our transience. So, keep on searching and striving, and look out for a light at the end of the tunnel.

Glossary

I've listed only the surfing terms and the few nautical or scientific expressions that appear in the book. Linguists and other curious readers may refer to *The Encyclopaedia of Surfing* for a detailed treatment of its history, slang and folklore.

A

aerial, to ride a surfboard into the air off the face of a wave, then landing back on the same wave.

aerial 360, to perform a 360° rotation on your board whilst carrying out an aerial.

air drop, to fall through the air after popping up, rather than remaining in contact with the face of the wave.

ankle-basher, the smallest size of surfable wave.

B

backside vertical re-entry, a short-boarding manoeuvre – the surfer looks over their blind shoulder from the base of the wave, shoots up its face vertically, then pivots their board through 180° and drops back down.

barrel, an alternative word for a tube.

beating, to be held underwater and pummelled by a breaking wave – as in 'taking a beating' – and sometimes also to be pounded into and dragged across various obstacles on the seabed.

Bing, a brand of surfboard founded by Bing Copeland in 1959.

bodyboard/bodyboarder, a surfer who rides a torso-sized wedge of foam under their chest. Note that there are two very different classes of bodyboarder: children and adults who seldom stray out of their depths, and **brassnecks** who wear short swim fins and attempt to ride steep, hollow breaks that might be death to stand-up surfers.

bong, a water pipe used for smoking cannabis.

Bonzer, a five-finned board invented in Australia by the Campbell Brothers, who still make them. Also, an Australian colloquialism for something (or someone) which excites admiration by being outstandingly good of its kind.

booger, a bodyboarder.

bottom turn, a turn made at the base of a breaking wave that enables the surfer to travel parallel to its face.

break, a place in the sea where waves suitable for surfing are formed.

brassneck, a bodyboarder.

bummed out, to be frustrated, disappointed.

C

Chinese gybe, a sailing term for an accidental gybe.

clean-up set, a set of waves larger than the surfers at a peak are waiting for, which break further out to sea and wash them towards the shore.

close-out, a wave that breaks along its entire face, or sections of its face, at once rather than peeling either left- or right-handed.

cockroach, to be pinned down on the seabed by a breaking wave and wave one's arms and legs about.

cut-back, a sharp turn of 90 degrees or more, that takes the surfer back to the shoulder of the wave if they have travelled too far in front of it.

D

ding, a dent or hole in a surfboard.

Diplock, Chris Diplock, surfboard shaper and owner of the eponymous brand.

dropping in, to take off on a wave that someone else is already surfing, both a breach of etiquette and very dangerous, as the act risks high-speed collisions between surfers.

F

fin, a foil on the underside of the tail of a surfboard that provides side force, like the keel of a yacht, and stops the board from skidding or sliding. A thruster has three fins, a Quad four, and a Bonzer five. Longboards usually have a long, single fin.

Fish, a split-tailed, twin-finned surfboard, invented by Steve Lis in California in 1967, initally ridden as a kneeboard.

foamy, a surfboard for beginners built from Styrofoam or similar. Some brands of foamy, notably the Costco Wavestorm, have cult followings, see: https://www.newyorker.com/news/sporting-scene/the-cult-of-the-costco-surfboard

G

goofy foot, to stand on a surfboard with your right foot forwards.

H

Hang Five, a longboarding manoeuvre. The surfer walks to the front of the board while riding a wave and sticks the toes of one foot over its nose and into the sea.

hang loose, to relax, chill out – sometimes accompanied with a *shaka* sign. Both its origin and meaning are disputed. In nineteenth-century England, the phrase was slang for letting your testicles swing freely, and was an invitation to relax, or a celebration of relaxation. In Hawaiian custom, the *shaka* is a gesture of friendship.

Hang Ten, a longboarding manoeuvre. The surfer walks to the front of the board while riding a wave and sticks the toes of both feet over its nose and into the sea.

head plant, to wipeout and land on your head.

Hobie, a brand of surfboard named after its creator, Hobart Alter, one of the first to build surfboards out of fibreglass and foam; also responsible for the Hobie Cat classes of catamarans. Hobart passed away from cancer in 2014; his brand is still extant.

hodad, to visit the seaside without going surfing; to take a surfboard to the beach without using it.

Hula, a traditional form of Polynesian dance.

I

isobar, a visual representation of surface pressure. Tightly packed isobars on a chart show a storm.

K

kick out, to exit the wave you've been surfing by riding up its face and over its crest.

L

left-hander, a wave that breaks from right to left when you have your back to it. Easier to ride for goofy footers.

logger, a longboarder.

longboard, a 7–11 foot surfboard. It's easier to catch a wave on a long board, as their extra length enables their riders to paddle faster. They are also more stable than shortboards, but less manoeuvrable.

line-up, two or three points on land that are used as markers by surfers to determine their position in the sea.

M

man in the grey suit, a shark.

Mini Mal, an abbreviation of mini Malibu – a short (7–8 foot) longboard.

N

nose riding, surfing a longboard with one or both feet on the nose of the surfboard. See also **Hang Five** and **Hang Ten**.

nose water, a sudden and unexpected discharge of seawater from the nose, which gets forced into the sinuses while surfing, and takes its time to escape.

O

offshore, a wind blowing from the land to the sea, and into the faces of the waves, sometimes with sufficient force to delay their breaking for a fraction of a second.

onshore, a wind blowing from the sea to the land. Onshore winds cause the swells to break prematurely and unevenly. Waves are easier to catch in onshore conditions, but less satisfying to ride.

osmosis, damage caused to a surfboard after a ding, by water that has been absorbed into its foam core.

P

pearl, type of **wipeout,** named after pearl divers, who descend to great depths on a single breath. When a surfer pearls, they bury the nose of their board in the face of the wave that they're trying to ride, which forces them under it.

point break, a surf break that wraps around a promontory, whose size is sometimes augmented by refraction.

pop-up, a surfing manoeuvre – to rise from lying prone on your board to upright when you catch a wave.

R

rails, the edges of the surfboard, usually curved like the leading edge of an airplane's wing to generate lift.

right-hander, a wave that breaks from left to right when you have your back to it. Easier to ride for regular footers.

rip/rip tide/rip current, a current formed by the water from broken waves returning to the sea, usually running perpendicular to the shoreline.

regular foot, riding a surfboard with your right foot forwards. The opposite of goofy foot. About three quarters of surfers are regular footed. There's an easy way to find out whether you're regular or goofy foot if you haven't surfed, skated, or snowboarded before: sit on the ground with your knees bent and feet flat on the ground. Take hold of one end of a rope with both hands, and ask someone else to pull you up with the other end of the rope. Whatever leg you choose to stand on first will determine your orientation.

S

shaka, a Polynesian hand gesture. To make a shaka, extend your thumb and pinky on one hand, curl the other fingers into a ball, then waggle your hand to and fro.

shoulder, when a wave rises up and starts breaking, the shoulder is the unbroken part of its face closest to the breaking part.

short board, a surfboard 5–7 feet in length, designed to be highly manoeuvrable on the face of the wave.

sponger, a bodyboarder, named after the soft foam surfaces of bodyboards.

spoon, a type of surfboard, so named because of its broad and rounded nose, which tips upwards from the horizontal when the board is laid flat.

SUP, a stand-up paddleboarder. SUPs ride long wide boards, which they stand up on at all times. They carry a paddle to propel themselves, and practise their sport on flat water as well as surf swells.

stick, slang for surfboard.

surfboard, wave-riding machine without any moving parts. Most surfboards are built with a foam core and a fibre-glass skin. The core starts as a blank – a slab of synthetic honeycomb, which is planed into shape. The foam is then draped in fibreglass cloth, which is trimmed to fit, then sealed around the board with resin. Fin boxes are cut into the core to hold the fins that give the surfboard lateral drive.

T

tombstone, when a surfer is trapped underwater, and their board on the surface above is pulled upright by the leash attached to their ankle so as to resemble a tombstone.

tow-in surfing, a big-wave surfing technique whereby the surfer is towed by a jet ski onto a breaking wave. The surfer then releases the tow rope and rides the wave. Noted for the strong bonds between the jet-ski drivers and surfers, who often swap roles, one towing while the other rides, then vice versa.

train/wave train, a technical term for the manner in which the frenzy of waves around a storm consolidate themselves into groups of different sizes as they travel across the ocean.

trim, to adjust the balance of a surfboard fore and aft by moving your weight backwards and forwards.

TWD, True Wind Direction, measured in degrees from the direction in which you are heading. o degrees TWD is in your face and 180 degrees TWD is at your back.

U

undertow, an imaginary current believed to drag swimmers underwater and drown them.

V

Venturi effect, when an incompressible fluid travels through a narrow aperture, its speed increases and its pressure drops. The phenomenon was first noted by and is named after Giovanni Battista Venturi, Italian physicist.

W

white water/white water zone, the turbulent and frothy water created when a wave breaks, which has enough energy to carry a surfer into shore. Beginners learn to surf on these broken waves, in the white water zone where they occur.

wipeout, to fall off a surfboard. See also **pearl, cockroach, head plant** and **tombstone**

Picture credits

Chapter 1: Gale at Eype, Dorset. The waves in the picture are three to five metres tall (Iain Gately).

Chapter 2: Headstone in the graveyard of St Andrews, Church Ope Cove, Portland (Iain Gately).

Chapter 3: St Perran's cross in the dunes behind Perranporth beach (Wikimedia Commons).

Chapter 4: *Bathing in Brighton* by George Cruikshank, from his 'Comic Almanac for 1836'. The baby on the right-hand side of the engraving is about to get tubed.

Chapter 5: Surfer duck-diving under a wave (Willyam Bradberry/ Shutterstock).

Chapter 6: Chart of Lyme Bay (Iain Gately).

Chapter 7: Engraving of diatoms (Wikimedia Commons).

Chapter 8: Wave breaking over house at Broad Street, Lyme Regis (courtesy of Lyme Regis Museum/ www.lymeregismuseum.co.uk).

Chapter 9:   A goofy foot surfer performs a backside bottom turn (Staffan Rennermalm/Alamy Stock Photo).

Chapter 10: Surf Snowdonia's wave garden in Dolgarrog, Wales (image courtesy of Surf Snowdonia/www.surfsnowdonia. com).

Chapter 11: Surfboard shapes, from fish (left) to longboard (right) (Katerina Pereverzeva/Shutterstock).

Chapter 12: A percebes collector on a reef beside the pinnacles of Cabo Ortegal (Xulio Villarino/www.xuliovillarino.com).

Chapter 13: Mick Fanning performs a roundhouse cutback on a small wave (courtesy of Rian Castillo/digitizedchaos.com).

Chapter 14: Broadbench, Kimmeridge, in offshore conditions (Dan Hunter/https://hunterfoto.smugmug.com/Latest-work).

Chapter 15: La Graciosa seen from Caleta de Famara (Iain Gately).

Chapter 16: Sandwich Islanders (Hawaiians) playing in the surf, 1841 (Wikimedia Commons).

Chapter 17: Surfer bailing out of a close-out (*High fly* by Dani Nemeth/www.daninemeth.com).

Coda: Croyde, looking back into a breaking wave (Zac Gibson).

Glossary: Sir Pellias, by Howard Pyle, from *The Story of King Arthur and His Knights*, Charles Scribner's Sons, New York, 1903.

Acknowledgements

My thanks to Tim Knight for the inspiration; to John Eastham, Will Cooper, and Miles Dann, for companionship along the way; to JMC and Manuel in Caleta De Famara; to Ed Wilson for his indefatigable advocacy of my cause; to Richard Milbank for his editorial excellence, and to Georgina Blackwell for her skill and patience in shaping the manuscript for print.